QUICK-TIME HOMEMADE BREAD AND PASTRIES

REAL HOMEMADE YEAST BREADS, ROLLS, AND DOUGHS MADE SIMPLE, IN LESS TIME

MARY ELLEN WARD

Copyright © 2019 Mary Ellen Ward
All Rights Reserved

All rights reserved. No part of this publication may be reproduced, distributed, or transmitted in any form or by any means, including photocopying, recording, or other electronic or mechanical methods, without the prior written permission of the publisher, except in the case of brief quotations embodied in critical reviews and certain other non-commercial uses permitted by copyright law. Requests should be made via the contact information found at the website below.

www.thehomemadehomestead.com

Of the chief helpers, observers, and learners in my kitchen, my daughter Olivia is at the top of the list. She strives to be a leader in all that she does, but knows enough to learn from those with experience, too. Though bread making is still low on her checklist of accomplished kitchen endeavors, I hope that this book might be for her what it is intended to be for you: A guide to make baking good, wholesome bread less daunting, and an avenue to learn an enjoyable new culinary trick or two.

Happy Bread-Baking, Olivia. I'll take the Cranberry-Apple.

INTRODUCTION

The first bread-making book I wrote is one titled, Your Daily Homemade Bread: Easy Stand Mixer Bread Recipes: Best Basics (to which there is also a second companion book in the series, Your Daily Homemade Bread: Easy Stand Mixer Dough Recipes: Bagels, Rolls, and Sweet Treats). The books have been well-received, and some excellent feedback has been had from an excellent set of readers. Like myself, those readers have been happy to have finally found a way to make healthful, wholesome, cleaner bread and dough creations that are simplified, take less time (that most precious commodity!), and fit more easily into this busy, modern life.

The basic method used in the recipes in the *Daily Homemade Bread* series is a true time-saver for people who own stand mixers, like the well-known Kitchenaid® mixer. The trouble is that those targeted books leave out a whole other group of home bakers and potential home bread bakers: people equally pressed by life, but who don't own a stand mixer. And so here we are, ready to fill the void. This book was written expressly for those people — people looking for an easier, faster, better way to make bread at home, but without the expense or bother of using a large stand mixer. The same method that makes stand mixer bread faster and easier can be applied to making bread by

Introduction

hand. All it takes is some conversion. That is what this book has done for you.

EATING CHEAPER, CLEANER, *BETTER* FOODS

There's a story I've been known to tell, that goes a little something like this:

A couple of summers back, my family took a trip up north on summer vacation. We stayed in a lovely little cabin on a quiet, pristine lake as the guests of some truly wonderful family members. We did all the normal things vacationing camp families do — we roasted marshmallows for s'mores and did lots of simple cooking to maximize our relaxation time. Hot dogs and hamburgers were steady lunch and dinner choices, and so upon arrival, I went to the local grocery store and stocked up, which of course included the rolls. As it happened, we didn't go through all the rolls on vacation and, waste-not-want-not, some unopened packages of hot dog rolls traveled home with us and were subsequently stashed up on the pantry shelf and forgotten. For weeks.

I happened back upon these gross little buns one day and that's when I realized that they looked the same as the day I bought them. I'm talking NO mold. No green fuzzies. No whites or blues or interesting colors. Nothing to indicate they hadn't just come home that very day. They didn't even *feel* hard in the package.

Naturally, I was a bit weirded out by these freakish rolls. I mentioned it to the kids, who also knew (being primarily eaters of fresh, home-baked breads) that real food SHOULD rot. Good bread SHOULD turn interesting colors. Our curiosity piqued, this became something of a challenge. We let the offending rolls sit up on that shelf, waiting to see how long it would take before this commercially-manufactured bread-like product would do what real bread does and start to mold and harden.

School started and homemade breads and rolls came and went...most eaten, usually, still warm and crushed by the bread knife of my too-

Introduction

impatient eldest son, *("It's fresh bread out of the oven! How do you expect me to just let it* sit *there!?")*. Some went to the chickens after turning stale after several days. Some became croutons and breadcrumbs. And yes, some were pushed to the back reaches of the cabinet and, sadly, turned interesting hues. Those darn hot dog rolls, though, *still looked and felt like the day I bought them!*

We let those hot dog rolls sit in a corner from August to December (no exaggeration) AND THEY NEVER GREW MOLD. They didn't really even harden. From the bag, they felt almost as soft as any other bag of rolls on any grocer's shelf. Now naturally, this begs the question: *What in the world are they putting in these rolls to make them eternally soft and incapable of molding??*

Clearly, some sort (or more likely, multiple sorts) of mold inhibitor, preservatives, and dough conditioners were present in these rolls. Added chemicals that serve no purpose other than to ensure that cheap commercial bread producers don't have to provide a fresh product at all in order to provide a "fresh" appearing product, which can remain on store shelves for indefinite periods of time. These are just not things I need in my family's bread, especially considering that bread, when it's all tallied, makes up a significant part of the typical household diet. Really, if you were to improve only one product in your family's diet for the health of it, and wanted the most "bang for your buck" impact, bread products would be an excellent place to put your time.

One leading classic commercial white bread, very typical of grocery store breads, lists 20 separate ingredients. Compare that to the Everyday White Bread recipe in this book, which lists a grand total of six (flour, water, salt, sugar or honey, yeast, natural fat or oil).

BUT OF COURSE WE ALL *PREFER* REAL BREAD!

It really isn't much of a sell to convince people that it's better and more enjoyable to eat fresh-baked breads on a regular basis. Who wouldn't rather eat a loaf of warm comfort? But we all know why we don't: homemade breads take a lot of time. Honestly, bread baking is intimi-

Introduction

dating to many people, despite the fact that up until relatively recently it was considered a simple chore; a part of life.

By now, however, most of us probably were not taught by our homemaker mothers and grandmothers to bake bread as previous generations were. Time got in the way. Life got in the way. We settled, and the commercial grocery companies ran rampant with what was once a simple, wholesome food. So many of us would like to take back some of these better old ways, but those pesky things like jobs and bills and time-takers keep getting in the way. This is exactly what birthed the stand mixer book series. That series provided the essentials for home bread baking that was manageable and fit into a modern lifestyle so that it *could* be, once again, a staple of a healthy household's diet.

What makes the stand mixer breads so "doable" is in part the handiness of the tool — the stand mixer; but what actually makes those breads so manageable is the method and ingredients employed. Really, it comes down to just one ingredient: the yeast. The recipes in this book almost exclusively utilize a rapid-rising yeast which speeds up not just the time it takes to make the bread rise, but also the entire process, shortening it a great deal. There are some basic rules to using fast-rising "instant" yeasts, but once you know them and understand the basics of how this yeast functions, the method itself is easily replicated and it becomes almost routine to make bread using this method.

THE BASIC BREAD METHOD THAT SIMPLIFIES HOMEMADE BREAD BAKING

There's a good reason that the process in this book is different, and that it actually works (and works so well). It's the yeast.

IT'S ALL ABOUT THE YEAST (A PRIMER ON FAST-ACTING YEASTS)

With a couple of (very easy) exceptions (some favorite no-knead recipes chosen strictly for their hands-off ease, speed, and *fabulous flavor!*), the recipes in this book all use "instant" yeast. Using instant yeast changes the traditional bread-making process, eliminating rise periods, increasing yeast activity (thus increasing bread-baking *success*), and seriously shortening the time it takes to make a great loaf of homemade bread.

Instant yeast is not a product that is as well-known to home bakers. It's not even that easy to find in all grocery stores unless you know what you're looking for. That's why this discussion, while perhaps not the most stimulating of your day, certainly deserves a few minutes of your time. It will clear up a lot of unknowns and confusion about the types of yeasts that are out there and how they should be used.

Active Dry Yeast is the type of yeast that is most familiar to most of us. This is the traditional granulated dry yeast that is found most commonly in strips of three small packets on nearly any grocery store shelf. It can also be found in small jars (typically four-ounce size) and in larger vacuum-packed bricks and jars. Active Dry Yeast, or "ADY" as it is often referred to, needs to be dissolved in warm water in a range of 100-110 degrees Fahrenheit. It does not perform particularly well outside of this range (either above or below — below will stagnate the yeast and keep it from getting going and above will kill the yeast before it can do its job for you); and so a thermometer is recommended when using active dry yeast. Recipes using ADY traditionally require two separate periods of rising and resting, drawing out the time from it takes to make a batch of bread from start to finish.

Instant Yeast is the other mainstream yeast option, and it is a very good one for us modern bakers with more and more strains put on our time. Instant Yeast is also granulated, but the granules are much smaller than those of ADY, and the yeast itself is more active to begin with than ADY. These smaller granules are much more capable of absorbing water and liquids, and so Instant Yeast does *not* need to be started by dissolving or proofing it in water. In fact, it should not be proofed because it gets going so quickly that if you do proof it in water, you will lose the gases and action that you want to be captured by your bread dough to make that wonderful loaf of perfectly-raised bread. When you bake with Instant Yeast, you pitch it right in with your other dry ingredients and just give it a quick stir through to distribute. (*Traditional bakers often question whether the instruction to mix the instant yeast in with the dry ingredients is correct; it is!)

Instant yeast also does not require such long and drawn out periods of rising and resting. It needs only one short time to rest after you first mix the ingredients together, and one much shorter period of rising between shaping and baking the loaf (as opposed to multiple periods of resting and rising in traditional bread recipes using ADY). In addition, liquid temperatures for recipes in which Instant Yeast is used are higher; their range is more toward the 120 to 130 degree Fahrenheit range (this is because the more active yeast likes a little bit higher temperature but also because the other ingredients will help take some of the heat and the warmer liquid gets things up and running quickly, speeding along your dough-making process). Also, because the other ingredients help to buffer the temperature of the hot liquids to the yeast, I find that when you bake with Instant Yeast the temperature range isn't quite such a touchy subject, and something a bit one side or the other won't usually do any harm. As a side note, $120\text{-}130^0$ is what hot tap water in American households is normally set to (unless you've gone against the advice of hot water heaters, code, and plumbing professionals), so it's fine to just use the hot water straight from your hot kitchen tap.

To sum it up, looking at the two types side-by-side, using this Instant Yeast method saves you quite a bit of time and hassle. Compare the two processes:

Active Dry Yeast

1. Dissolve yeast in warm water
2. Wait until yeast is foamy and active to use (5-10+ minutes)
3. Mix together dry ingredients
4. Add dissolved yeast and water mixture/fats/wet ingredients
5. Mix thoroughly
6. Turn out onto floured surface and knead for 6 to 8 minutes
7. Let rest and rise until doubled (about 45 minutes to one hour)
8. Punch down dough
9. Shape dough and place in pans
10. Let rise until double (again, about 45 to 60 minutes)
11. Bake (approximately 25 to 30 minutes)

Total Est. Time (including 10 minutes for measuring, mixing, and shaping): 137-179 minutes or about **2h 20m to 3h**

Instant Yeast

1. Mix together dry ingredients *with* the Instant Yeast
2. Add water/liquid and fats all together
3. Mix
4. Turn out onto floured surface and knead 6 to 8 minutes
5. Let rest for 10 minutes
6. Shape dough and place in pans
7. Let rise until doubled (about 30 to 45 minutes)
8. Bake (approximately 25 to 30 minutes)

Total Est. Time (including 10 minutes for measuring, mixing, and shaping): 83-103 minutes or about **1h, 20m to 1h 40m**

Not only is the Instant Yeast method cutting your work down by about 30%, but even more importantly, it's reducing your *time* by almost *half!* What many of us find once we start working with instant yeast is that this gap tends to widen because the yeast is more active and rises more consistently in shorter time than ADY does. When you start getting into recipes like dinner rolls and Italian and French loaves, which have a tendency to rise even more quickly, you'll find you can reliably get a nice loaf of warm bread ready for dinner in an hour or less — no kidding!

RapidRise™ and Bread Machine Yeast, although not our two main yeast players per se, definitely deserve some mention here, and here's why: They're really the same thing as Instant Yeast. Why does this matter? Because in many locations you might not be able to find Instant Yeast (particularly if you shop in stores that don't cater as well as they should to the home-baking crowd); but you usually *will* be able to find either RapidRise™ or Bread Machine Yeast.

RapidRise™ Yeast is nothing other than the yeast giant Fleischman's brand name for their trademark Instant Yeast. *It's just a brand name but it's still Instant Yeast!* You should note, though, that even Fleischman's doesn't limit themselves to the trademarked name and they also sell instant yeast that is labeled as just plain instant yeast. It tends to come in much cheaper bulk packages like one-pound vacuum bricks and it's usually more available through outlets like online grocery, Amazon, and wholesale shopping clubs (Sam's Club, BJ's, etc.).

Bread Machine Yeast, by any company, *is just instant yeast*. It sometimes has added ascorbic acid to help condition the dough, but it's Instant Yeast. The fact that it is Instant Yeast is what allowed those bread machines that were popular through the end of the last millennium to work — because the yeast granule was small in size, good at absorbing liquid, and could be thrown into the mixer along with everything else.

Bottom line when you're out shopping for your yeast? Buy whatever is most affordable and most available to you under any Rapid-Rise, Bread Machine, or Instant Yeast label. But here's a tip: If you plan ahead and shop online or at a wholesale club, you'll find greatly reduced prices. One pound can cost you as little as four ounces does in the grocery store and you can always break larger bulk packs down into smaller jars, storage containers, or baggies, and pop them in the freezer to keep until you need them in future.

STEP BY STEP QUICK-TIME BREAD BAKING METHOD

If you have some experience baking yeast breads and doughs, by now you've noticed some distinct differences in the process. If you have no experience that's okay, too; it might be an advantage to you, as this is the method you'll have learned from the beginning. Whether you're an experienced bread baker or not (maybe you're the one who, like myself years ago, put it off because that long and drawn out process always seemed so daunting?), in no time at all you'll have this routine process down and then you'll find it easy to recreate or try new recipes because the process itself changes little if at all; the differences lie primarily with the ingredients.

That breakdown we saw in that previous table? That's pretty much your process in an eggshell:

- Measure out your dry ingredients and softened fats or oils,

including your yeast. Give all a quick stir through to distribute the yeast and other ingredients.
- Add in water at around 120F. Stir to combine until ingredients come together to form a ragged ball.
- Turn the dough out onto a floured surface. (For most recipes it's okay if you have some dry remnants left in the bottom of the bowl — they'll mix in as you knead. If it seems like *too* much dry matter and the dough is too dry and rough, add a little water; just don't make it too sticky.)
- Knead the dough for about 6 to 8 minutes until a smooth ball is formed. Do this by folding the dough over, pushing down, turning one-quarter turn and folding and pressing repeatedly until a nice dough ball (that is not very sticky) is formed. Don't get too caught up in the process of kneading — something pretty close will do and it's not an exact science where one-quarter turn as opposed to one-half turn will make or break you; just follow the basic method, keep it consistent, and work the dough evenly throughout.
- Cover the ball with a piece of plastic wrap sprayed with baking spray or a damp cotton towel (my personal wallet-friendly, environmentally-friendly preference).
- Let dough rest for 10 minutes.
- Shape the dough into appropriately-sized loaves and place in a prepared pan to rise, covering with greased or oiled plastic wrap (baking spray works well) or a damp, lint-free kitchen towel.
- Let rise as directed and then bake.

NOT SO SET IN STONE

Bread baking and yeast dough baking is a little different than other types of baking because it doesn't always follow the instructions to the letter. This is probably why people are more afraid of it than they should be — because you have to leave a little more to experience and instinct, and we like things to be more predictable than that. However, we shouldn't let this scare us away from what is really an easy process, and that results in one of the most time-honored and favored of all home-baked products.

So, what's the point here? The point is just that we must accept that everything cannot be precisely timed or laid out in a bread or dough recipe. The same exact recipe made in two different kitchens will act a little differently. The end result might vary a little, but more to the point, it might just take you a little bit of a different process to get it there. Environmental factors have noticeable impacts on baking bread. Your kitchen might be a little cooler or warmer than the average; so, your dough might take a little more or less time to rise. Your flour brand might be a little more compact than another; so, your recipe might take a little more water to get it to come together. Maybe your kitchen is drafty, so you need to be a little creative to make a comfy place for your dough to rise (try a cardboard box over your covered pans, or heat your oven to warm with a pan of hot water on the lower rack, shut it off and place uncovered loaves inside to rise — just be aware that they often rise quickly this way! In fact, it's a great way to speed up rising when time is crunched!).

You'll even see differences within your own kitchen from season to season. I live in New England where the winters are cold and dry and the summers can be quite hot and humid. Rising isn't much of a problem in July, but in dry January I have to pick and choose my best rising locations. (A table which happens to be placed above a kitchen heater is a big help!). You may even experience rising and bread baking getting easier over time; that stands to reason as you become more comfortable and experienced, but there are also other reasons; the more you bake bread at home, the more yeast that is in your kitchen environment, and the easier it can actually be to rise and bake bread!

What we're getting at here is that you should expect to personalize your bread baking experience. Enjoy that experience and know that you're not doing it wrong if you have to tweak or change an ingredient amount or a rising time, or maybe, even, a baking time (because all of our ovens are different, too). These things are no big shakes and you're sure to handle them just fine. Nothing is ever set in stone with bread, but nothing is too difficult to deal with, either.

HOW AND WHEN TO ADD FATS AND A BIT ABOUT FAT SUBSTITUTIONS

This is a question that comes up more often than you might think: What is the best time to add the fats into a recipe?

As long as you've added your fat in before the "stir and mix until dough comes together in a shaggy ball" stage, the bread won't be too particular. You want to add your fat in at a stage when it can be evenly distributed. The best time for this depends somewhat on what type of fat you are using and whether it is a solid or a liquid fat. Although the recipes in this book do specify a particular fat, substitutions for matters of preference are perfectly fair game; so, before we talk about the best time to add the fat, let's chat about fats and substitutions.

Most home cooks and bakers have a fat that they are most fond of for their various cooking and baking projects. In my home, for example, we believe in traditional eating and believe in the nutritional benefits of lard and butter, their ability to both provide and carry vitamins and fat-soluble nutritional compounds, and our bodies' own abilities to recognize and process them. Although we do use oils as well, in baking I tend to steer more towards one of these traditional options.

Vegetable, canola, and olive oils, and butter are the most common fats found in bread recipes. But other types of fats, including shortening, butter substitutes, and good, old-fashioned lard, are options, too. The bottom line is that whatever fats fit your dietary needs or beliefs are the fats that you should use when you make your bread. For the most part, fats substitute back and forth easily in bread making. To work a substitution, all you need to do is replace the fat listed in the recipe with the same measure of the fat you want to use. I can't really guarantee that it will work in the case of every last fat possibility, or that you will not see some small difference in the outcome (flavor, weight or texture, for example), but I've never run across a fat that didn't work, either.

In answer to the question of when to add the fat: First off, solid fats like butter, shortening, and lard should be softened so that they are workable. If they are still semi-hard or have some solid state to them, the best time to add them is with the flour and dry ingredients (probably best before the yeast is pitched in or after yeast is stirred through, only so that it doesn't stick to the solid fat and keep ingredients from distributing throughout the dough). Liquid fats (oils or melted butter, etc.) can go right in with the dry ingredients, too. A third option, the one I like best, is to measure the fat into the hot water once you've measured the water. This way, it distributes throughout easily along with the wet ingredients and in the case of more solid fats like butter, lard, and shortening, they soften or melt and become easier to work.

Really, bread isn't that picky in terms of things like this as long as the ingredients get a fair distribution. The process of kneading the bread for six to eight minutes acts as a good deal of the mixing process and helps ensure that more even distribution, anyway.

SHAPING THE LOAF

Another little something that people ask about quite frequently is how to shape the loaves once the dough is ready. It's a discussion that's easily taken for granted. There are a couple of options and some methods that seem to work just a little better for breads made with instant yeast. Of course, many experienced bakers have their own favorite methods and as we like to say, nothing is set in stone, so if you already have a method you prefer do feel free, but let's take a quick look at some methods.

Hand-shaped loaf. What I refer to in this book as "hand shaping" is simply forming a basic loaf shape that roughly fits the length and width of your loaf pan. Most recipes in this book make two loaves of bread, so in this case, you would divide your ball of dough after it has rested into two equal parts, and then gently pull them into an elongated loaf shape. Tuck any ragged sides or ends to the underside of the loaf and gently pinch if necessary to seal the bottom of the bread and "hide" cut and ragged edges. As the dough rises, these will weld together and seal.

Of course, because the bread dough will be rising, it will not be as tall as your loaf pan when you first shape it — more towards halfway full in the pan. It should just about reach end-to-end and side-to-side in your pan, though; if it's not an exact fit, don't stress. As the dough rises and settles it will grow to fill the pan as long as it is close in size, and the pan will help to form your rising loaf. Pans should be treated (greased or oiled) prior to laying the dough in to rise *(*do note — there is an exception to this for a couple of recipes, such as those cooked in Dutch ovens so read through your recipe instructions!)*. For prepared/greased pans, it's best to put your dough in top-side-down first, and then turn it. This gives the top side a quick, easy greasing so that it doesn't stick to your covering as it rises.

Hand shaping can also be used for larger, longer loaves like French and Italian breads that are baked on a baking sheet or flat stone. Simply follow the same basic method, using the length of the pan as your guide and just take care not to stretch the dough to the point of ripping. With all dough-shaping methods, you want to work the shape via *stretching*, without *ripping*. I tend to use the hand-shaping method more when I'm in a hurry and don't want to take the time to roll and shape the loaf. It works very well, although I do find the rolled loaves tend to rise better and have a bit of a better texture.

Rolled Loaf. As mentioned, rolled loaves are probably the best way to go. The rise and texture are generally more reliable in loaves shaped with the rolled method. It is especially useful when you want to make a filled or flavored loaf, such as a Cinnamon Swirl or cheese-filled breads. It is also how you would start the shaping of cinnamon and sweet or savory rolls.

To shape your bread loaf by rolling it, first divide the dough as instructed after it has rested for the ten-minute period (do let it rest the full ten minutes or you will be fighting the dough's natural elasticity and forming the loaf will be difficult). Take each piece and push and pat it into a rectangular shape (you may use a rolling pin if you prefer). The length is not very important; do whatever the dough responds to without ripping. The width, while not critical, is more important so that when you finish rolling your piece it will fit nicely into your pan. The typical bread loaf pan is 8 ½ inches long, so make your rectangle for a regularly-sized loaf 8-8 ½ inches wide by about 14 to 16 inches long (again, the length is less critical). (Note — if you are filling the bread, such as with cinnamon sugar or savory meats and cheese, this is the time when you would spread that filling. Simply spread fillings all over the surface of the dough, leaving about a half inch of clear dough space along the entire outside border.)

Starting with the short end, roll the dough up all the way. Your rolls should be fairly tight to decrease air pockets and deep swirls in the bread that can keep the dough from rising into a cohesive loaf. Do expect, though, that if you have spread a filling over the dough before rolling it (such as for a swirled, filled bread), some air pockets are not uncommon. You just want to avoid having your roll be too loose and creating large air spaces that fall apart when slicing. No worries, practice makes perfect. When you have rolled the entire loaf end-to-end, tuck the long seam and the sides to the underside and pinch the seam to seal the loaf. Place the loaf top-side-down in the greased loaf pan, turn right-side-up, and cover to rise.

Rounds. Round loaves are shaped much the same way as hand-shaped loaves; you simple pat and pull them into a round shape. Pinch the seams to the bottom to seal and hold the shape. Depending on what you want your dough and loaf to turn out to be, the pinched seam can be placed at the bottom of the loaf (if you want a smooth, rounded top — do this for bread bowls and smooth-topped round loaves) or you can turn the loaf so that the pinched seam is placed to the top, where it will often split open a little for a nice artisan effect. Done in miniature, this is a good way to make dinner rolls without having to learn a whole new recipe. If you place them fairly close together in the pan you will get a rounded-topped pull-apart type roll; spaced apart the entire surface will brown and harden as single rolls that resemble mini-loaves or hard rolls — a great way to change up a tried and true bread recipe! You can do this with almost any bread recipe and then simply space the loaves/bread bowls, et cetera out on a baking sheet. A good option if you don't have the right loaf pan or not enough for the amount you want to bake!

Other shapes. Bread is pretty versatile in terms of things like shape and loaf size. If you keep in mind that you may need to adjust baking time relative to your new loaf shape/size, most recipes let you do whatever you want with them. From braids to boules there are many different shapes that bread is formed into. While we won't delve into all of them here, if there is a shape or size you want to try and the recipe seems to be up for it, give it a go! Give Google a glance or check out shaping videos on sites like YouTube. You might come up with something quite impressive!

BASIC EQUIPMENT AND INGREDIENTS TO GET YOU STARTED

The beauty of baking bread at home from scratch is that the equipment and ingredients required are so very minimal. As far as equipment goes, all you really need is:

- A large bowl capable of fitting about eight cups of ingredients with enough space left for stirring and working the dough.
- Sturdy mixing spoons (good wooden spoons will do the job well!)
- A cleanable flat work surface (if you don't mind flouring and working directly on your counter, it's perfect!) or
- A large cutting board or
- An optional baking mat designed for working and rolling doughs
- Bread loaf pans
- A couple of good knives: a sharp, flat-bladed knife is helpful for slashing loaves if desired and of course you will want a good serrated bread knife to partake of your delicious dough creations!

Some things that come in handy, but are not necessary for success, include:

- Large cotton/linen kitchen towels (what are often called "flour sack towels" work particularly well — they are cheap enough that you won't mind doing the dirty work with them and are large enough (about two feet square) to be used for a variety of bread- and dough-making tasks.
- A stainless steel bench scraper – very helpful for dividing dough, scraping off surfaces, and lifting loaves into pans. They're even very helpful for cleaning up the mess afterward.

Ingredient needs for most loaves are very basic. In fact, once you've sourced the instant yeast you probably already have what you need for most of the recipes in this book (maybe even all of them). Your grocery list will look something like this:

- Instant Yeast (or bread machine yeast or RapidRise™; plan about 1 ½ tablespoons per two-loaf batch)
- Flour (about 6 ½ Cups per batch)
- Salt
- Sugar or another preferred sweetener (see substitution section for more)
- Butter, oil, or other preferred fat

So you see, the requirements to make great bread at home in quick time, practically any time, are minimal. Grab that Instant Yeast and go!

BREAD PAN FAQ'S

Another easily overlooked discussion is that of bread pan requirements. This, too, is a question asked frequently. What's nice is that these doughs and recipes work well with even slightly different size loaf pans, and, what you already have is going to work just fine. For the average kitchen, there is no need to go out and invest in anything new and your pan should return an excellent result even if it varies in size by a half-inch or an inch.

That being said, the loaf pan size that most of these recipes have been tested with is your standard 9x5 bread pan. Some manufacturers like to tweak things, so you might find that what's in your cabinet is something like an 8 ½ x 4 ½ or a similar close size. It won't matter. Your bread will rise and fill the space and unless it is grossly undersized it'll work just fine. If the pan is a little on the longer side, your loaf may not rise as tall, but it won't make a noteworthy difference.

Glass or metal? This seems to be a common baking question, but once again, the answer comes down to this: Which do you own? Which do you prefer?

I tend to amass baking supplies and so I do happen to own both, and I do use both. I personally prefer metal over glass and I even, in this case, prefer a regular metal baking loaf pan to cast iron (I'm a fan of cast iron and so I do own a couple of cast iron bread pans, but they don't give me the best result). My personal experience has been that heavier loaf pans like glass and cast iron take longer for the bottom to bake and so you'll often end up with lighter, more moist bottoms (not really the goal for yeast breads) with darker tops. It's not that it's a great difference and perhaps your experience with your oven will be different, but if I am lending advice, I say go with a good, standard, metal loaf pan and don't go out of your way to over-invest in bread pans.

Baking Sheets. Baking sheets come in very handy for baking homemade bread. Not every loaf or recipe wants to be baked in a loaf pan. French-style breads, Italian bread, rolls, and buns will need something larger and more capable of free-form freedom. Regular cookie and baking sheets fit the bill just fine. For some things you might prefer a pan with sides if you like the softer, crowded effect — pull-apart rolls, sweet, and savory rolls, for example; a good old standby 9x13 cake pan will suit you here just fine (maybe a couple of them).

Dutch Ovens. Dutch ovens are my exception to cast iron vs. metal for bread baking, but only for specific recipes. Artisan loaves and often sourdough breads do very well in cast iron Dutch ovens. Dutch ovens mimic the steaming action of specialized European bread ovens and help you achieve that crusty, airy, chewy European-style texture. The no-knead recipes in this book utilize baking in a Dutch oven and the results are a fantastic, super-simple bread that tastes like you patronized a high-end bakery! In this instance, cast iron really is recommended, because it can take the high heat necessary for these types of breads while regulating the temperature for an even bake without burning. You can easily get away with some variation in the size of your pot, so if you have one, use it, and don't run out for new. If you do not own a Dutch oven yet, this just might be the best reason for you to buy one. If purchasing, I'd recommend an eight-quart Dutch oven. Honestly, if you were looking to invest in one piece of baking equipment to help you make great homemade bread with little effort and top-notch results, put your money into a Dutch oven and try the artisan-style loaves.

(*Note — the only recipes that specifically mention Dutch oven baking are the artisan loaves, but you can use a Dutch oven for baking other bread loaves, too. Use your discretion in terms of breaking the dough down into smaller loaves or not, depending on your Dutch oven and batch size.)

INGREDIENT SUBSTITUTIONS OF INTEREST

We've covered fat preferences and substitutions in good depth, but there are some other basic ingredient substitutions of interest to discuss before we get baking.

Flour Substitutions. Questions about changing out flours are one of the most common in terms of substitutions. In our more health-conscious environment, many people prefer a more whole-grain bread, and so the question of whether you can simply exchange a whole-grain flour for a white flour comes up. In simplest terms the answer is yes, but...

First, let's talk for just a second about the flour that is called for in the recipes in this book. The primary flour used in these recipes is run-of-the-mill All-Purpose Flour. Of course, some recipes are very specific recipes...a 100% whole wheat recipe, for example, or an oatmeal bread, or multi-grain bread, but by and large, the base flour used is white all-purpose. The reason for this is that all-purpose is the most affordable and most available flour, and the one most people are likely to have in their pantry or cabinet, and first and foremost the intent of this book is to make wholesome, homemade bread baking affordable and achievable in the weekly scheme of things. It is also because refined white flours lend us a flavor and texture that we really enjoy (much as that may be taboo to admit in this day and age!).

This being said, you can and should experiment with the flour that you like best, whether that be for reasons of dietary preference or for matters of brand or type preference or similar reasons. The recipes will give you the starting point for proportions. Generally speaking, if you are switching out one type of flour for another you should start with an equal measure exchange. In other words, if a recipe calls for 6 cups of all-purpose flour, use 6 cups of your flour instead.

What you need to be most aware of when exchanging flours is that different types of flours act differently in a recipe. White flours and refined flours more easily absorb liquids and are usually less dense and result in a faster, easier, more reliable rise. It is pretty common to have to keep adding incremental amounts of additional flour in order to get the dough to come together and be workable (this is a major contributor to the density of whole-grain breads); and so, you simply cannot always expect the result to be exactly the same when exchanging flours. The result might be a smaller loaf or one that requires more rising time, for example.

An option that is usually better than completely replacing one flour with another is to replace a portion — up to half — of the white flour with your desired flour. In most recipes, this will turn out a slightly different bread but will preserve the liquid absorption and easier rising ability of the white flour, while bringing the flavor and/or dietary benefits of your preferred flour into the bread.

Another option is to try using one of the less refined, whole grain white flours that have come onto the market, and/or using this flour in a half-and-half combination.

Bread flour, while still a refined white flour, is a good option as well. It can really help turn out nicely-rising, nicely-textured bread loaves. In fact, it's probably a better option than regular all-purpose flour, but bread flour is harder to find, is more expensive, and tends to be less readily available in larger-sized bags. If it is readily available to you and you don't mind paying a little more, this might be the right option for you. Simply prepare the recipes with the bread flour as you would with all-purpose flour.

Something else to consider (not a flour but a supplement to flour that can make a big difference) is Vital Wheat Gluten. Vital Wheat Gluten is a naturally-occurring protein additive. It is already in bread flour (this is really the basic difference between regular flour and bread flour) and is used in bread baking to enhance rising and texture. It generally results in a better-rising, lighter loaf. You can add Vital Wheat Gluten to any type of flour (a typical recommendation is to add two to three tablespoons to the flour — less if the dough becomes too soft or spongy). Vital wheat gluten can really be a help when using denser whole grains and whole wheat flours. It is also recommended if you live at a higher altitude and have a hard time getting your breads and doughs to rise.

One final flour type worth a mention is high-gluten flour. The King Arthur Flour Company of Vermont, for example, makes a high-gluten flour option (they call it 'Sir Lancelot') that is often preferred by professional bakers and chefs who use King Arthur because the higher gluten content lends that rising and texture advantage. The King Arthur Company is just one example; there are numerous other producers of high-gluten flour out there (it just so happens that King Arthur resides in New England, as do I, and so they are a notable, accessible option for me). King Arthur and other high-gluten flours can be harder to find in grocery stores, but you can order online direct from the company(ies) and through online retailers like Amazon. The point is, you might have to really look for it or source it, but high-gluten flour can be a very good bread-baking option that you can use just like all-purpose but with a better result. If you know of a local food cooperative ordering group or if you have access to a kitchen or baking supply vendor, you might be able to find a superior product like this at an extremely reduced bulk rate, which can be very economical if you start making most or all of your own bread on a regular basis.

Substituting Sweeteners. Refined sugars in the diet are another popular mainstream concern, and so sweeteners often become another question and subject for substitution. The upside of this discussion, to begin with, is that you are not usually looking at a lot of added sugar content as an ingredient in homemade bread (a few tablespoons at best in most cases, and several recipes included that require no additional sugar at all). The equally good news is that it's easy to substitute out white sugars in bread recipes.

Very basically, to make a substitution for a sweetener, use an equal amount of natural sweeteners or alternative sugars in the recipes given. For example, if a recipe calls for three tablespoons of white sugar, use three tablespoons of honey instead. Some one-to-one sweetener substitutions include:

- brown sugar
- honey
- molasses
- maple syrup
- maple sugar
- corn syrup

The one thing to be aware of when working these substitutions is that if you substitute a liquid sweetener for a dry sweetener, you may need to adjust the amount of liquid you are using in the recipe. Start by backing off the liquid measure by an equivalent amount and add more liquid if the recipe is too dry. You can also add a small amount of flour in increments if the resulting dough is too wet or sticky. Either way, it's an easy correction to make.

Artificial sweeteners are not recommended as substitutions in bread baking because the yeast needs the sugar as its fuel source. Natural sugars feed the yeast and this "digestion" is what results in the rising action. Without sugar sources, the yeast cannot feed and act. Flour does naturally contain some sugar, but it is limited so if the yeast needs to rely on the available sugar conversion in the flour it will act very, very slowly — too slowly for what you want for most recipes (the exception being no-knead recipes because they have a very long rising time). If sugar is a concern for you, the best recommendation for most recipes is to *reduce*, but not eliminate, the sugar or sweetener (a reduction of about ⅓ the measure is probably the most you want to attempt). Very slow-rise recipes like no-knead breads and sourdoughs do not, however, need additional sugars and so for the more sugar-conscious bread baker, these are the best options for excellent, reliable, breads with full texture and flavor.

As is only logical, any substitution away from the original recipe ingredients and measures will change the end product as compared to the original result. This doesn't make it less or poor; most often the resulting changes are minimal and would never have been known if you weren't aware of them or looking for them. More often, the result is better, or just...different. For example, when you replace white sugar with molasses, you get a nice, deep, darker flavor. Is that better? If you like deep, richer flavors, then yes. If you're a white bread purist like my eldest, not as much. The bottom line? Bake what you like. Like what you bake. Expect some variation. Do a little experimentation to find what you like and feel best about. Enjoy it!

One of the biggest advantages of making your own bread and dough products at home is that you have total control over the ingredients that you put into them. You can source that flour from a company you've researched and really trust. You can use a GMO-free flour, or an organic flour or sugar if that is what is most important to you. You can remove or replace an allergen, do away with preservatives, and you can save a tremendous amount of money over similarly-prepared commercial products. Baking bread and doughs at home not only allows you a sense of pride in a job well done but also a sense of control and security in knowing the products you've put into your food; and so yes, if that substitution is important to you, give it a try and feel great about the change that you've made for you and yours.

THE LIFE OF HANDY HOMEMADE BREADS

Remember that little story at the beginning about the little hot dog rolls that could? (Never die, that is.) Well, your bread *isn't* that. And oh, how grateful you should be.

It's good to know what to expect in terms of shelf life from your breads so that you can plan and bake accordingly, especially if you are working to make homemade breads a major part of your household's diet. Without commercial preservatives to lend them a shelf life to last the ages, your fresh-baked homemade breads cannot be expected to last for weeks and months. If we had to put a number to it, I'd estimate your wholesome bread's shelf life (at normal, dry, room temperatures) to be about five days. That is, five days without molding and growing interesting growths and colors.

"Day-old bread" was always a thing — a reduced-price thing — because the quality starts to deteriorate in fresh-baked products relatively quickly. A day won't make these breads "bad." A day doesn't make much of an impact on them at all, really. After two to three days (if your loaves have lasted that long) you can usually expect your bread to see some noticeable change in moisture and texture...a little drier, maybe, but still good sandwich bread and definitely good for toast. It's when you get too much past this, toward five days, that you're likely to really see a decline in your bread and want to refresh your batch, or find an alternative use for it (bread pudding! French toast! Croutons!).

Having said this, again, you have to consider where you live and at what time of year you're baking. Five days in winter here in my pantry? No problem. In July without refrigeration? A science experiment.

Different loaves and recipes react differently and have different useful shelf lives, too. Moister breads hold up longer but can run mold risks more quickly. It's a case-by-case basis you'll sort out as you go.

GETTING AHEAD BY BAKING AHEAD

We accept that great bread doesn't come with a shelf life of months. We embrace it for what we're trading off (preservative junk). We've got a good quick-time bread-baking method to help us out, but maybe you feel like you need to be able to stretch the time between bakings a bit more. So, what are your options for prepping ahead and doing more while you're at it?

First, let's understand this: The thing with Instant Yeast is that it acts so fast that it's not the best yeast product to use for doughs that will be made ahead and/or frozen. It can work, and it's not terrible to throw an extra dough loaf in the freezer and give it a try to see how it works out for you, but often what happens is that the yeast rises too much in the initial stages and doesn't save enough life to finish the rise after the thaw; and so the dough and resulting loaf can be stunted. It's worth a try, but more likely to work better for things like dinner rolls and bread bowls where a solid rise might be less critical. If you try freezing bread dough made with instant yeast, don't let the rise get too much of a start. Let the rising complete as part of the thawing and rising preparation process for baking the dough after it has been frozen.

These breads do, however, freeze well as finished products. If you are looking for a make-ahead, prep-ahead option, you are better off baking the product from start to finish and freezing the finished product, tightly wrapped. If you do bake ahead and freeze breads for another day, be sure to cool them all the way out before wrapping so that they do not sweat and get soggy. Also, wrap and freeze them as soon as possible after cooling to preserve the best quality and freshness possible.

Finally, there is a middle ground that works well as a make-ahead option with instant yeast breads, and that is par-baking (partially baked). Par-baking is a sort of middle ground between freezing dough and freezing finished product. When you par-bake, you make the bread all the way through, rise it, and bake it, but you *under-bake* the bread and finish baking it another day when you want it. The advantage of par-baking is that you get the convenience of prepping ahead and having bread on hand, but you preserve the best fresh-baked features and get to eat a warm finished loaf. (Incidentally, this is also a good way, with or without the freezing part, to prep fresh bread ahead for a party or a holiday when your oven might be otherwise occupied until the last moments and still be able to serve fresh, warm bread!)

If you choose to par-bake your breads and freeze them for later, bake them to a point where they are no longer raw or uncooked in the middle. It's often recommended to reduce your baking temperature by about 25 degrees and to cut back the baking time by about 25% (for most recipes in this book, try 15 minutes at a temperature of 325^0F). If you take internal bread temperatures, the goal would be around 180-185^0F, but basically, you want to bake the loaf until it starts to just turn a very light color on the outside. After baking, let the loaf stand for about five minutes, then turn it out onto a cooling rack and cool completely before wrapping and freezing.

When you want to use your par-baked bread you can bake it either from a frozen or a thawed state. If frozen, start the process at a reduced temperature for about 10 minutes, then increase to full temperature until nicely browned. If thawed, bake at full temperature until browned, which will not take as long as it would for a loaf made all the way through from dough to loaf (typically around ten minutes, but check after the first five minutes of baking). A pan of hot, steaming water (boil a tea kettle and fill the pan in the oven) is a good addition to help keep the loaf from drying out.

DAUNTLESS BREAD BAKING

If there is one thing I have tried to do with my books, it is to remove the obstacles to good, clean, home-cooked and home-baked goodness. Our grandparents, for all their simplicity and limited budgets, ate *well*. So much better than we eat today. And they did it with the simplest of ingredients, with some knowledge and ability, and without the health and dietary issues that plague our society today.

Amongst the biggest hurdles I see, and in fact, admittedly, I've experienced myself in times past, is the fear of baking good, traditional foods like bread. It mystifies us. It looks hard. We've lost what our grandmothers knew. We're sure it won't come out like the world-class French baker's products on Main Street and we're a bit self-conscious about even trying. You know what? That is okay. Who cares?

Bread baking was never a very hard thing, but it was a time-consuming thing and that's how these things got lost in translation as our lives got crazier and crazier, and that is the gap I've strived to bridge with this and other books I've offered. I've tried to bring to you processes that turn out a great product in a timeframe more suitable to the dual-worker families of today. Equally important, I've tried to encourage people to not feel so intimidated by good food. Yours may not be the bread of the French baker; mine is not, either. But yours *can* and *will* be *yours*. It will be bread that you have put yourself into for the nourishment and enjoyment of you and yours. It will be bread that you have chosen specifically for you and yours. It will be bread that you have substituted, squeaked and tweaked to be food that you want to eat and that you feel right about feeding to others.

It may also be bread that didn't rise. It may be bread that you used unsalted butter in that really didn't work out and tasted pretty bland. It may be bread that you made on a day that was cold or with yeast that was old that just wouldn't flourish and grow. It may be bread that the chickens enjoyed and saved you a couple of scoops of grain. (Do I sound like I speak from experience here?)

Sure, you'll have batches and experiments that don't work out. Sure, you'll get distracted and burn a loaf. Sure. You might "waste" some or a few bucks in ingredients, but I can almost guarantee that you *will* see success — more often than not, you'll see success. You shouldn't be afraid to try. That one success is only a couple of hours and a batch of simplified bread away, so let's see some recipes and let's see what you can do!

THE RECIPES

MEASUREMENT ABBREVIATION KEY & HELPFUL EQUIVALENTS

The abbreviations for measurements in this book (which follow standard U.S. baking measurements) are as follows:

- Tablespoon: TBSP
- Teaspoon: tsp
- Cup/Cups: C
- Ounce/Ounces: Oz
- 3 tsp= 1 TBSP
- 1 ½ tsp= ½ TBSP
- 2 TBSP= ⅛ C or 1 Oz
- 4 TBSP= ¼ C or 2 Oz

LOVELY LOAVES

FARM HEARTH WHITE BREAD

We all have that one bread that is our go-to favorite. In my house, it's this simple, delicious, traditionally-styled white bread that I've dubbed "Farm Hearth" because it reminds me so much of Grandma's farmhouse bread and the comfort of hearth and home. This is a bread and a process so simple that soon you will know it by heart and baking it will become second-nature...just the way it always seemed baking family favorites was for Grandma!

- 2 ½ C hot water, about 120^{0}F
- 3 TBSP butter, cut into chunks
- 6 ½ C Flour
- 3 TBSP granulated sugar
- 1 ½ TBSP instant yeast
- 1 TBSP salt

Measure out the hot water and add the butter to the water to soften as you prepare the dry ingredients. Set aside.

Place all dry ingredients, including the yeast, into a large mixing bowl. Stir through a few times to distribute dry ingredients evenly.

Pour in the water and butter and stir to combine. Mix until the dough begins to come together and forms a fairly uniform ball. Dough may still be a bit shaggy at his point, but as long as most of the dry ingredients have incorporated your dough is ready for the next stage. If too much flour and dry matter remains in the bottom of the bowl, add a little more water (by the tablespoon). If the dough is too wet, sprinkle a bit more flour into the mix.

Turn the ball of dough out onto a floured surface and knead for 6 to 8 minutes, until a smooth and elastic dough is formed. If necessary, work in more flour as you go.

After kneading, cover the ball of dough and let the dough rest for 10 minutes.

While the dough rests, prepare two standard loaf pans by greasing with shortening, lard, or baking spray. When the dough has rested for 10 minutes, divide the ball of dough into two equal halves and form the dough* into two shaped loaves. Place each loaf into a prepared pan, turning once to coat the top; this will help keep the dough from sticking to the covering during rising. Cover the loaves with a clean, damp towel or oiled plastic wrap and let the bread dough rise in a warm place until doubled (about an inch above the rim of the loaf pan).

Bake at 350°F for 20-25 minutes, until nicely browned. If desired, brush with melted butter immediately upon removing loaves from the oven to give the crust a softer top and a nice sheen, adding a butter-top flavor. Let the bread rest and firm up in the loaf pan for 2 to 3 minutes, then remove to a baking rack to cool.

*To form dough, you may simply shape each half of the dough by hand into a general loaf shape, or you may pat each half into a long rectangle (8x14) and then roll up, starting with the short end; place in pans so that the seam is on the bottom of the loaf for rising. Both methods work nicely, but the rolling method tends to give a nicer, more even, better-rising loaf.

THE VERY VERSATILE FARM HEARTH WHITE BREAD

The basic Farm Hearth white bread dough also serves as a great base for a variety of other top-notch baked products. Besides the bread itself being an excellent traditional loaf, the versatility of the dough is the other main reason I would choose this as my one and only if I had to choose one.

Cinnamon Swirl Bread: Prepare dough as for white bread. For this loaf you will use the "rolled" loaf shaping method. Divide dough in half, then press or roll each half into an elongated rectangle, about 8x14 inches. Cover the dough all over with a strong cinnamon-sugar mixture, leaving about ½ inch clear around the edge of the dough. If desired, sprinkle with walnuts or raisins as well. Starting with the short end, roll the dough into a loaf shape and pinch the seams to the underside to seal. Bake at 350^0F for 25 minutes or until done. *(Here's a tip! If you don't need two white loaves each time you make your Farm Hearth white bread, use one half of the dough to make a cinnamon swirl loaf!)*

Dinner Rolls: Prepare dough as directed for white bread loaves. Grease two 9x13 baking pans (or line with parchment paper). Pinch off dough to make rolls about two inches round and smooth them into balls. Place rolls in pans so that rolls are almost touching, leaving just a small amount of space to rise (balls will rise into each other and rise up in pull-apart fashion; if you prefer bun-style fully-crisped crusts, space the rolls out on a cookie sheet and leave rising space so that they will not touch). Cover and rise until doubled (approx. 25 minutes). Bake at 350°F for 20 minutes or until done.

Sandwich Rolls or Burger Buns: Prepare dough and divide into about 14 even balls. Smooth balls into rounded, slightly flattened roll shapes and place the balls and on a greased or parchment-lined baking sheet, leaving room to rise without touching. Cover and rise until doubled. Bake in 350°F for 20 to 25 minutes. If you prefer softer tops, brush with melted butter while still hot. For crustier rolls, leave untouched or brush with a beaten egg white prior to baking. Cool on a wire rack, cut in half, and serve.

Pizza Crust: Prepare dough and divide into two or three equal parts (two for a thicker or larger, sheet-size pizza, three or more for round, smaller, or personal-size pizzas). Oil your baking sheet. Sprinkle with cornmeal (optional). Press each ball to the sides of the sheet, pressing and working without ripping the dough. Before topping it is best to bake each crust for about 10 minutes in a 375°F oven (this prevents soggy pizzas). Remove par-baked crusts from oven, top as desired, return to oven, and bake until cheese melts and slightly browns and the pizza is done (about 20 minutes).

Bread Sticks: Prepare dough and divide it into two equal balls. Grease two large cookie sheets. Sprinkle with cornmeal (optional). Pat each ball out to fill the baking sheet, but do not rip. Use a smooth-edged knife, bench scraper, or pastry cutter to cut down the center of the dough lengthwise; now work down the pan and cut at one-inch intervals widthwise down the pan. For more flavor, you can brush the dough with olive oil and sprinkle with desired toppings. Sea salt, onion or garlic powder, shredded cheddar, parmesan, or mozzarella cheese, sesame seeds, or herbs, used alone or in combination, are all good choices. Cover and let rise to about ⅓ height. Bake at 375°F for 17-20 minutes.

Garlic Knots: Prepare dough. Divide into 24 to 30 balls. On a lightly floured surface, roll each ball into a short, fat rope, rolling back and forth to elongate into a workable length. Tie each "rope" into a single knot and place on a greased or parchment-lined baking sheet. Cover and let rise until a little under doubled in size. Place on greased baking sheets and bake at 350°F for about 15 minutes, or until done. While knots are baking, melt one cup butter with three or four cloves minced garlic or three teaspoons garlic powder and set aside. When knots are baked through, remove from oven and let them cool for a few minutes until they firm up a bit and can be manageably handled. Dip each knot, completely covering each in the butter mixture, and place on a baking pan to set. Best enjoyed warm.

Cinnamon Rolls: Prepare dough as directed but increase sugar to four tablespoons and increase the instant yeast to two full tablespoons. Use butter as your fat instead of lard or oil. Divide the dough into two equal balls. Work one ball at a time and roll or pat the ball flat on a lightly floured surface, making a rectangle that is about 10x14 (measure does not need to be exact). Spread very soft butter over the entire surface and then sprinkle generously with cinnamon sugar (generous with the cinnamon!). Starting with the long side, roll the dough into a long log and place the seam on the bottom. Cut the log into 1 inch rolls and place them on greased or parchment-lined baking sheets, close but not quite touching, leaving space to rise (if you do not like your rolls touching and want a clean edge on them, space them out so they do not rise into each other during rising or baking; alternatively, you can place each roll in a large [oversized] muffin tin). Cover and let rise until almost doubled in size. Bake at 350°F for 20-25 minutes, until lightly browned. Allow to cool slightly before glazing. As they cool, mix a glaze of powdered sugar and milk to desired consistency and drizzle over tops. Best if served warm.

Bread Bowls: Prepare dough as for bread loaves, but do not shape into loaves. Divide into six or eight even balls (depending on how large you would like your bowls — they will double in size). Grease two baking sheets or line with parchment paper; shape balls into small round loaves, and place the rounds on the prepared sheet, spaced with plenty of room to allow them to rise to double *without touching* (you want each "bowl" to have a solid crust; if they touch they create a soft spot when pulled apart). Let rise until almost double in size. Bake in a preheated 375°F oven for 20-25 minutes. Let bowls brown more than usual for a firmer crust. Bread bowls should be left to cool for several hours before using, or even overnight (in a cold oven uncovered or in a large paper grocery bag is a good way to preserve the firm crust...best not to store in plastic). When ready to use, cut flat across the top about 1/3 of the way down, low enough to make a good-sized opening. Pull out the soft interior and use bread bowls to serve soup, chili, etc.

Fried Dough: Prepare dough as normal. Divide into several balls (these can be any size you like; just keep the size of your frying pan/vessel in mind when making them). Pat or stretch each ball to make it flat (aim for something about ½ to 1-inch thick — it will puff up as it fries, too). Heat fry oil or lard to around 360°-370° (when a tiny ball of dough sizzles when dropped in, the oil is ready). Carefully place flattened dough portions into the hot oil and fry until golden brown on both sides, turning once during cooking (about 2 minutes total).

CRANBERRY-APPLE BREAD

There is a beautiful thing about Cranberry-Apple bread. Its delicious simplicity. You're sure to notice that this bread is not a lot different than the Farm Hearth White Bread. The addition of chopped fresh apple pieces and dried cranberries turn regular white bread into a real treat. Infinitely versatile, use this bread for toast, French toast, a unique pairing for sandwiches, cold meats and cheeses (it's turkey's favorite sandwich base!), hot open-faced style holiday sandwiches, or an upgrade to your dinner bread. You'll never regret giving this easy, scrumptious bread a try! (P.S. this is an excellent bread choice if you enjoy good, old-fashioned bread pudding!)

- 1 green apple, washed, unpeeled, cored and diced into small (¼ inch) pieces
- 2 ½ C hot water, 120^0 F
- 3 TBSP butter, cut into chunks
- 6 ½ C flour
- 3 TBSP granulated sugar
- 1 ½ TBSP instant yeast
- 1 TBSP salt
- ½ C dried cranberries (sweetened or unsweetened)

Core and chop the apple and set aside. Measure the hot water and add the butter to the water to soften as you prepare the dry ingredients. Set aside.

Place all the dry ingredients, including the yeast, into a large mixing bowl. Stir through a few times to distribute dry ingredients evenly.

Add the prepared apple pieces and the dried cranberries. Stir through to distribute once more.

Pour in the water and butter and stir to combine. Mix until the dough begins to come together and forms a fairly uniform ball. The dough may still be a bit shaggy at his point but as long as most of the dry ingredients have been incorporated, your dough is ready for the next stage. If too much flour and dry matter remains in the bottom of the bowl, add a little more water (one tablespoon at a time). If dough is too wet, sprinkle a bit more flour into the mix.

Turn the ball of dough out onto a floured surface and knead for 6 to 8 minutes, until a smooth and elastic dough is formed. Work in more flour if the dough is too sticky.

After kneading, cover the ball of dough and let the dough rest for 10 minutes.

While the dough rests, prepare two standard loaf pans by greasing them with shortening, lard, or baking spray. When the dough has rested for 10 minutes, divide the ball of dough into two equal halves and shape into two loaves*. Place each loaf in a prepared pan, turning once to coat the top; this will help keep the dough from sticking to the covering as it rises. Cover the loaves with a clean, damp towel or oiled plastic wrap and let the dough rise in a warm, draft-free place until doubled (about an inch above the rim of the loaf pan).

Bake at 350° for 20-25 minutes, until nicely browned. If desired, brush with melted butter immediately upon removing loaves from the oven to give the crust a softer top, nice sheen, and add a butter-top flavor. Let bread rest and firm up in the loaf pan for 2 to 3 minutes, then remove to a baking rack to cool.

*To form dough, you may shape each half of the dough by hand into a general loaf shape, or you may pat each half into a long rectangle (8x14) and then roll up, starting with the short end; place in pans seam-side down. Both methods work nicely, but the rolling method typically results in a more even, better-rising loaf.

AMISH-STYLE WHITE BREAD

Amish-style breads have considerably more sugar in them than typical white bread recipes. This makes for a sweeter-tasting bread, but the sugar also provides plenty of "food" for the yeast, which in turn makes this bread an almost fool-proof fast riser – often needing only a half-hour to rise. It is a very good bread for beginners who want to get their bread-making legs under them. It is also a good choice if you find conditions in your kitchen make rising bread difficult. The bread pairs beautifully with almost anything, is an excellent breakfast, brunch, or sandwich bread, and makes a versatile base as a dough for flavored sweet breads, sweet rolls, or buns. Do note, this recipe makes ONE loaf.

- 1 C milk
- 4 C all-purpose flour
- ⅓ C sugar
- 1 TBSP instant yeast
- ½ tsp salt
- ⅓ C soft butter
- 2 eggs, lightly beaten

On your stovetop or in your microwave, heat the milk to between

120°F and 130°F. Set aside and let cool slightly to between 115 and 120°F.

In a large mixing bowl, combine the flour, sugar, salt, and instant yeast. Stir through to combine. Add the cooled milk, butter, and eggs and mix to combine until dough starts to come together as a ball.

Turn the dough out onto a well-floured surface and knead for about 8 minutes. After kneading, cover the dough with a clean linen cloth and let rest for 10 minutes.

While the dough is resting, prepare a loaf pan. Grease the loaf pan.

When the dough has rested, shape the dough into one loaf shape and place in the pan, seam-side down. (Dough can also be used for making dinner rolls – divide evenly into balls and place, spaced, in a greased or parchment-lined 9x13 baking pan or in greased muffin tins.) Cover dough with a damp linen towel or oiled/sprayed plastic wrap and let rise in a warm, draft-free place until doubled.

Preheat oven to 375°F and bake for 20 to 25 minutes or until golden brown. If desired, coat top with butter while still hot for a soft top and nice shine.

*To form dough, you may shape the dough by hand into a general loaf shape, or you may pat into a long rectangle (8x14) and then roll up, starting with the short end; place in pans seam-side down. Both methods work nicely, but the rolling method typically results in a more even, better-rising loaf.

HONEY WHEAT BREAD

Wheat bread not only offers a nice change-up from the routine of white breads, but it offers quite a lot in the way of health benefits, too. A source of whole grains, wheat breads are considered better for you. A completely whole-grain bread offers the most dietary benefits; however, 100% whole grain breads are often hard for people to fall in love with. They simply don't offer the softness and structure of white breads; for some people, the intense flavor can be a bit harsh, too. This Honey Wheat Bread recipe does contain white flour but is still more than 50% whole wheat flour, helping to increase your whole-grain intake and reduce refined flours in your diet. Cutting the flour with white flour results in a softer bread while moderating what some people perceive as a bitter flavor in whole-wheat breads. Further, because this recipe uses honey as its sweetener, this bread is just that much healthier still and the honey perfectly complements the wheat in flavor.

Much like the Farm Hearth White Bread, this basic honey wheat dough is a great one to use for dinner rolls and mini loaves.

- **2 ½ C hot water (about 120°)**
- **3 TBSP honey**
- **3 TBSP butter (or lard), cut into chunks**
- **3 C all-purpose flour**

- 3 ½ C whole wheat flour
- 1 TBSP salt
- 1 ½ TBSP instant yeast

Measure the hot water into a measuring cup and then add the butter and the honey to the water. Set aside.

Combine both flours, salt, and yeast in a large mixing bowl and mix through to distribute. Add the water, butter, and honey mixture into the dry ingredients. Stir just until dough forms and begins to come together as a ball.

Turn the dough out onto a floured surface and knead for 6 to 8 minutes. You want the dough to be of moderate firmness; the dough should not be hard (the ball needs to have some give and elasticity) but the dough also should not be sticky to the touch (a little bit tacky is okay at this stage, though). You may add up to an additional ½ cup of white flour if it is needed to reach desired consistency. If the dough seems too dry, add warm water by the tablespoon.

When done kneading, cover the dough with a clean towel and let rest for 10 minutes.

Grease two loaf pans while the dough rests. After the dough has rested for 10 minutes, form the dough into two loaves and place them in the prepared pans, turning each loaf once to coat the top to help prevent it from sticking to its cover as it rises. Cover the loaves with a clean, damp towel or oiled/sprayed plastic wrap and let rise in a warm place until doubled (about an inch above the rim of the loaf pan).

Bake at 350° for 25 minutes or until nicely browned. Lightly brush the tops of the loaves with butter while warm (if desired – buttering the tops adds flavor and helps to keep a softer outer crust).

*To form dough, you may shape each half of the dough by hand into a general loaf shape, or you may pat each half into a long rectangle (8x14) and then roll up, starting with the short end; place in pans seam-side down. Both methods work nicely, but the rolling method typically results in a more even, better-rising loaf.

COUNTRY RYE BREAD

Rye breads enjoy a popular following and are a top choice alongside white and wheat breads. Many people, even experienced home bakers, seem to feel daunted by rye bread, assuming it to be something complex and tricky. There is really no merit in this, though. What makes rye bread what it is, is simply the use of rye flour and a couple of complementary ingredients; the process is no different. In fact, rye bread often cooperates a bit better than wheat bread. It's really nothing to be afraid of, and, much like the honey wheat loaf, this rye bread recipe uses a blend of whole grain rye flour with white flour, achieving a health-boosted bread with great flavor and of moderate density, the way good rye bread should be. Brown sugar as sweetener helps to darken the color and flavor of the loaf for excellent depth. Rye bread lovers will rejoice with this easy, time-saving recipe!

- 4 C all-purpose flour
- 2 C Rye flour
- 2 TBSP caraway seeds
- 1 TBSP salt
- 1 TBSP instant yeast
- ¼ C brown sugar
- 2 C hot water (about 120°)

- ¼ C oil (or melted butter or lard)

Place all dry ingredients, including the instant yeast, in a large mixing bowl. Stir to distribute. Measure the hot water and add the oil (or butter or lard) to the water. Add the water mixture to the dry ingredients. Stir to combine, continuing to mix until dough forms and begins to come together as a ball. If dough is too dry to come together, add warm water one tablespoon at a time until there is enough moisture to let the dough hold together and be worked.

Turn the dough out onto a floured surface and knead for 6 to 8 minutes until the dough is smooth and elastic. Add up to an additional ½ cup white flour (a little at a time) if needed as you knead the dough to build proper consistency (moderately firm, not too sticky).

After kneading, cover and let the dough rest in for 10 minutes.

Meanwhile, prepare pans. This bread may be baked in regular loaf pans (will make two loaves) or may be baked on a greased or parchment-paper-lined baking sheet, formed into two round balls and spaced for rising (like a traditional round rye loaf). Slash the tops of the loaves prior to rising. Cover loaves with a clean, damp towel or oiled plastic wrap and let rise in a warm place until doubled.

Bake at 350° for 25 minutes, until nicely browned.

FARMHOUSE EGG BREAD

There are many reasons to make this Farmhouse Egg Bread an everyday standby. The egg adds additional protein and rich flavor, and a nice yellow color, too. The crumb structure is a little denser than normal white bread and so it is an excellent toast and sandwich bread, great for the kids' lunchboxes. Since the egg lends more moisture to the bread, it stays fresher longer. One tip – if you plan to use this bread as a sandwich bread, it's best to leave the loaf whole after cooling and wrap or bag it overnight before cutting. This helps the crumb hold its shape better when slicing.

- 2 C hot water (about 120°)
- 4 TBSP butter (or lard), cut into chunks
- 6 ½ C all-purpose flour
- 4 TBSP sugar
- 2 eggs
- 1 TBSP salt
- 1 TBSP plus 1 TSP instant yeast

Measure the hot water and then add the butter to the water to soften. Set aside.

Combine all dry ingredients, including the yeast, in a large mixing bowl. Stir through to distribute. Mix until the dough forms and begins to come together as a ball.

Turn the dough out onto a floured surface and knead the dough for 6 to 8 minutes. Add up to an additional ½ cup white flour (a little at a time) if needed as you knead the dough. You want the dough to be moderately firm, not too sticky but not too soft, either.

After kneading, cover the dough with a clean linen towel and let the dough rest for 10 minutes.

Meanwhile, grease two bread pans. After resting, shape the dough into two loaves and place in pans. Turn each loaf once in the pan to coat the top with grease and keep it from sticking to the cover as it rises. Cover loaves with a clean, damp towel or oiled plastic wrap and let rise in a warm place until doubled.

Bake at 350° for 20-25 minutes, until done. If desired, brush tops with melted butter for a soft, shiny crust. Let sit 2 to 3 minutes in the pans and then turn out onto a cooling rack. Let cool completely before cutting, wrapping, or bagging.

OLD FASHIONED POTATO BREAD

People really love their potato bread and this recipe will not disappoint even the biggest fan. Subtle and unique in flavor, this moist, firm bread is perfect for sandwich-making. It is yet another dough that is ideal for making dinner, burger, or sandwich rolls – imagine, homemade potato rolls! What's even better is that this recipe is a great way to use up leftover cooked potatoes – boiled, baked, or mashed, all are great candidates. (Remove skins, mash well, and use in equal amounts as called for in the recipe. Avoid heavily seasoned potatoes, but light seasonings like salt and pepper tend to disappear in the bread without a worry.)

If you are not using leftovers and you do choose to cook the potato to prepare this recipe, cooking two medium to large potatoes will net a cup of mashed potato. Reserve the cooking liquid and let cool to 120°F; use the reserved cooking liquid in place of the water in the recipe (if you do not have a full two cups of liquid left after boiling, use what you have and make up the rest with warm water). This will give you an even more robust potato flavor.

- 1 C cooked potato, mashed
- 2 C hot water (about 120°) or reserved potato water
- 2 TBSP butter, cut into chunks

- 6 ½ C all-purpose flour, plus one tablespoon to dust loaves before baking
- 3 TBSP sugar
- 1 TBSP salt
- 1 ½ TBSP instant yeast

Cook potato and mash well with a fork or potato masher. Set aside.

Measure out the hot water or reserved cooking liquid and add the butter to it to soften as you work the dry ingredients. Set aside.

Combine the flour, sugar, salt, and yeast in a large mixing bowl. Stir to distribute. Add in the mashed potatoes and mix lightly to distribute.

Add the liquid and butter mixture to the dry ingredients. Stir well to combine, stirring just until the dough forms and comes together as a ball. If the dough seems too wet, add flour a little at a time until a workable consistency is reached.

Turn the dough out onto a well-floured surface and knead the dough for 6 to 8 minutes until you have a moderately firm dough.

After kneading, cover the dough with a clean linen cloth and let the dough rest for 10 minutes.

Meanwhile, grease two bread pans. Divide dough in half and shape into loaves, then place in prepared pans, turning once to coat the tops. Cover loaves with a clean, damp towel or oiled plastic wrap and let rise in a warm place until doubled.

Just before baking, lightly brush tops of the loaves with water and dust lightly with additional flour.

Bake at 375° for 40-45 minutes, until done. Let rest in pans for 2-3 minutes and then turn out onto racks to cool.

HOMESTEAD HONEY OAT BREAD

Oatmeal bread offers both a flavor and nutritional benefit. Baking with oatmeal is a great way to get more whole grains in the diet, and it's kid-friendly, too; an excellent choice to boost your kids' bread nutrients. This bread comes out a bit sweeter, firmer, and slightly darker than most white breads, but not so dark as to be offensive to tried and true white bread lovers. It's a very versatile bread, excellent for toast, egg or chicken salad sandwiches, deli meats, and more. One final tip: if you like a darker oatmeal bread, substitute molasses for the honey in equal measure – a perfect dark bread pairing for barbeque, or just because!

- 1 ½ C hot water (about 120°)
- ½ C melted butter
- ½ C honey
- 6 ½ C all-purpose flour
- 1 C quick oats
- 2 tsp salt
- 1 ½ TBSP instant yeast
- 2 eggs

To top:

- 1 TBSP water
- 1 egg white
- Oats (either rolled or quick oats)

Measure out the hot water and then add the butter and honey to it. Set aside.

In a large mixing bowl, combine the flour, quick oats, salt, and instant yeast. Stir to mix through. Add the water, butter, and honey mixture to the dry ingredients and then add the eggs. Mix the ingredients through to combine until the dough begins to come together as a ball (dough may still be a bit shaggy).

Turn the dough out onto a well-floured surface. Knead 6 to 8 minutes until a smooth, moderately firm and elastic dough is formed. If dough is too sticky, work in more flour, up to another ½ cup.

Cover the ball of dough with a clean linen cloth and let rest for 10 minutes.

Meanwhile, grease two bread pans.

After resting, shape the dough into two loaves and place in pans. Turn the dough once in the pan to coat the top with grease and help prevent sticking as the dough rises.

Mix together the one tablespoon of water and an egg white. Beat lightly with a fork. Brush the mixture over the tops of the loaves and then sprinkle the coated loaves with additional oats.

Cover the loaves with a clean, damp towel or oiled plastic wrap and let rise in a warm place until doubled.

Bake at 375° for 40 minutes or until done.

WHOLE-GRAIN WHOLE WHEAT BREAD

Striving for 100% whole grain in your wheat bread? Here's your recipe! This recipe delivers a firm loaf with good moisture and structure and lots of wheat flavor. It is probably one of the more challenging recipes in this book, simply because that is the way of 100% whole wheat breads. Simply put, whole grains just do not absorb liquids or rise in quite the same way as more refined flours. True whole-grain breads have a lot to offer us, too, and this one is worth your time to perfect.

Just a note – this recipe makes only **ONE LOAF***.*

- 5 C whole wheat flour
- 1/3 C brown sugar
- 2 tsp salt
- 1 ½ TBSP instant yeast
- 2 C very warm milk (about 120°)
- 1/3 C oil

In a large mixing bowl, combine the whole wheat flour, sugar, salt, and instant yeast. Stir through to distribute dry ingredients. Add the oil and warm milk and mix through to combine until the dough comes together as a ball. Note that the consistency of this dough will need to be a bit on the wetter side; stay on the side of soft and just a little sticky with this recipe to maintain good end moisture and consistency.

Once the dough has formed, turn it out onto a well-floured surface. Knead for 6 to 8 minutes, until a smooth and elastic dough is formed. Cover the ball of dough with a clean linen cloth and let it rest for 10 to 15 minutes. (This dough can stand a little extra resting time, even as much as 20 minutes, because the rising action is slower, and this helps the wheat to absorb more moisture in the process.)

As the dough rests, grease a loaf pan. After resting, shape the dough and place it in the pan, turning once to coat the top. If you like, you may also form this into a round or oval loaf and bake it on a baking sheet. Cover the shaped loaf with a clean, damp towel or oiled plastic wrap and let it rise in a warm place until about 1 ½ times its size.

Bake at 375° for 40 to 45 minutes or until done. For a softer crust, brush the hot loaf with butter immediately after baking.

**If you're going to have trouble getting a bread dough to rise, it will be this one, and it's because of the whole wheat flour. You are more apt to find more variation between flour brands with whole wheat flour than probably any other; so if you are having trouble getting a good rise, first try a different brand of flour. Also, you can substitute half of the whole wheat flour with whole-grain white flour. Another easy problem-solving alternative is to add one or two tablespoons of Vital Wheat Gluten (available in some stores with baking goods or online) with the flour (tip: vital wheat gluten can help the structure of any problem bread!). If you do use vital wheat gluten, watch the moisture – you may need to add one or two additional tablespoons of milk or water. Finally, be patient with the rise – whole grain wheat is more finicky, so give it time in a nice, warm, draft-free space for best success.

SIX-GRAIN MULTIGRAIN BREAD

Multigrain bread is worth baking because it tastes great and has a lot to offer nutritionally, too. Generally speaking, as whole-grain options go, its flavor is more widely accepted than wheat bread. There's a bit more involved in the making of this bread and, much like whole-wheat bread, it may require a bit more patience with the rising. Still, with this simplified version this healthful bread is easy enough that you can enjoy it every day.

- 3 C all-purpose flour
- 1 C whole wheat flour
- ½ C bran
- 1 C rolled oats
- ½ C cornmeal
- ½ C unsalted sunflower or sesame seeds (personal preference)
- ½ C flax seed or chia seed
- 2 tsp salt
- 1 ½ TBSP instant yeast
- ¼ C melted butter
- ¼ C honey
- 2 eggs, lightly beaten

- **2 C very warm water (about 120º)**

In a large mixing bowl, combine white flour, wheat flour, bran, oats, cornmeal, sunflower seeds, flax, salt, and instant yeast. Stir through to combine.

Add the melted butter, honey, and eggs. Add the warm water. Mix together with a sturdy spoon and stir until ingredients are combined, and dough comes together as a ball.

Turn the dough ball out onto a well-floured surface and knead for 6 to 8 minutes. when finished kneading, lightly cover the dough with a clean linen towel and let the dough rest for 15 minutes (giving this dough a bit longer rest period gives the grains more time to absorb the liquid and results in a better rise).

Grease two loaf pans while the dough rests. After resting, form the dough into 2 loaves and place them in the greased pans, turning once to coat the top to prevent sticking (alternatively, because this bread is a lower-rising bread and a smaller loaf, you might prefer to make one large, round or oval loaf on a baking sheet or bake in a preheated Dutch oven – for Dutch oven baking instructions, see the no-knead bread recipes). Cover the loaves with a clean, damp towel or oiled plastic wrap and let rise in a warm place until a little less than doubled.

(Optional) Just before baking, if desired, combine one egg white with one tablespoon of water, brush it over the top of the loaves and then sprinkle with additional oats and/or sunflower seeds.

Bake at 350° for 35 to 40 minutes or until done.

FAST AND FAB FRENCH BREAD

There's really no reason not to make this bread. It is, hands-down, one of the most cooperative, easiest breads you will ever make. It almost never doesn't rise well. It rises faster than just about any other bread (something to keep in mind – keep a shorter watch and a closer eye during rising for this bread). It is also highly versatile, can easily be shaped and baked in mini-loaf style or used for bread bowls. It takes well to additions like meat and cheese. It pairs with all soups, pastas, or really any other meals and can typically go to oven within an hour for a fast and delicious supper side. Leftovers work well as sandwich and grilling breads and the loaves make great garlic bread, too. This bread is a tried and true fan-favorite and I've never met a person who didn't love it (warm, with butter, please!).

- 6 ½ C flour
- 2 TBSP sugar
- 2 tsp salt
- 1 ½ TBSP instant yeast
- 2 ½ C very warm water (about 120°F)
- 2 tablespoons oil
- Cornmeal (for baking pan, optional but recommended)
- 1 egg white, separated, lightly whisked for brushing the top

- **1 TBSP water, for brushing top**

Combine the flour, sugar, salt, and yeast in a large mixing bowl and stir through to distribute the dry ingredients. Add the warm water and oil. Stir until combined and dough comes together in a ball.

Turn the dough out onto a well-floured surface and knead for 6 to 8 minutes, until dough is smooth and elastic. After kneading, cover dough with a clean linen towel and let rest for 10 minutes.

Prepare the baking sheet while the dough rests. An 11x17 inch cookie sheet works well and will fit both loaves. (However, a little larger or smaller is fine, too; shape accordingly to fit the pan and if pans are very small use two sheets so that the loaves do not rise into each other. For pans shorter than 15 inches, place loaves diagonally). Grease the pan or line it with parchment paper and then sprinkle it with cornmeal.

After the dough rests for 10 minutes, divide the dough into two equal balls and shape. You can either pull the loaf into a long French-style loaf (about 15 inches in length), or pat the dough into a large rectangle (about 10x15) and roll, starting with the long side, to form a 15-inch long roll; pinch the ends and the seam together and lay seam-side down on the baking sheet. Cover the loaves with a damp towel or oiled plastic wrap and let rise until nearly doubled, about 30 to 45 minutes. (Note: you may also divide this dough into several pieces and shape it into small, individually-sized loaves.)

Just before baking, whisk together the egg white and the tablespoon of water. Brush the tops of the loaves all over with the water and egg white mixture. If desired, you may sprinkle the tops of the loaves with a bit of the cornmeal or with sesame seeds to make a Sesame French Bread.

Bake at 400°F for about 25 minutes, until done.

BASICALLY BAGUETTE

Baguettes have a reputation as being an impossible bread to bake, but there's really nothing especially difficult about them. The real challenge to baking baguettes at home is the lack of fancy steam-injected ovens that deliver the airy, soft inside texture while producing that hallmark crusty outer crust. This, too, however, is easily overcome with a little water bath in your oven. Now modify the traditional baguette recipe to fit the quicker and easier instant yeast method, and voila! You've now made delicious, crusty French baguettes in the comfort of your own home! You may even think it was easier than countless other types of yeast breads and pastries!

- 5 C all-purpose flour
- 2 TBSP sugar
- 2 tsp salt
- 1 TBSP instant yeast
- 2 C very warm water

In a large bowl, combine flour, sugar, salt, and instant yeast, and stir through to combine. Add the warm water and stir until mixed through and dough starts to come together. Note that baguette dough should be soft and airy – a wetter, stickier dough that just holds together.

Turn the baguette dough out onto a well-floured surface and knead lightly for about 3 to 4 minutes. Again, baguettes require less working and less firmness to maintain their open texture. After kneading, cover the dough with a clean linen cloth and let rest for 10 to 15 minutes.

After dough has rested, shape the baguettes. You can make this recipe into two longer loaves (about 22 inches), or three shorter loaves (about 15-inch loaves), depending on oven space and preference. To shape the dough, gently bring the corners into the center, pinch or press lightly, and then gently roll, stretch, and elongate into a thin tubular shape. Traditionally, baguettes have a tapered, pinched end.

Baguettes also tend to need support for their structure while rising. This can be achieved with a very well-floured linen cloth or in a baguette pan or form – whatever is available to you. Place the formed baguettes in the center of the cloth or form; if using a towel, place a fold between loaves and bunch the edges of the towel up to the sides of the baguette. Another option is to line your baking sheet with parchment paper with enough excess to create the folds and form. Parchment paper or a baguette pan may be preferable because you will not need to move the loaf onto the pan prior to baking after the dough has risen. To move the shaped loaves from a towel, gently roll them from the towel onto the pan.

Cover the formed baguettes with a damp cloth or oiled/sprayed plastic wrap. Let rise until 50 to 75% doubled. Using a baker's lame or a sharp, flat-bladed knife, hold the lame or knife at a 45° angle and make several slashes diagonally across the baguette.

Towards the end of the rising time, preheat your "steam" oven to 425°F. Place a heavy, oven-proof pan on the bottom of your oven or on the lowest rack of your oven and fill halfway with hot water. Leave this pan in the oven while it preheats and also while baking the baguettes. This creates the steam for the texture and crust. When loading baguettes into your oven, work quickly but carefully and close the door quickly to keep as much steam as possible inside the oven. Wear oven mitts to protect your arms from the hot steam, even when loading the cold pan.

Quick-Time Homemade Bread and Pastries

Bake baguettes in preheated, steamed oven for 25 minutes or until browned and done.

RUSTIC ITALIAN BREAD

What's pasta night without a warm slice of Italian bread to accompany? Less. But with this reliable favorite in your box of tricks, you can easily make it more. It's perfect for anything you'd want Italian bread for, including garlic bread. Twice as nice, this bread makes two sizable loaves so there's always plenty for a crowd, or if it's a quiet night in, freeze one to have on hand for later.

- **2 ½ C warm milk, heated to about 120⁰F**
- **6 C all-purpose flour**
- **4 tsp sugar**
- **1 ½ tsp salt**
- **1 ½ TBSP instant yeast**
- **¼ C olive oil**
- **Cornmeal (for baking pan)**
- **2 egg whites (for top, lightly beaten)**

Warm the milk to around 120°F (either on the stovetop or in a microwave) and set aside.

In a large mixing bowl, combine the flour, sugar, salt, and yeast. Stir to combine and evenly distribute the ingredients.

Pour in the warm milk and the olive oil. Mix until dough comes together in a ball. Turn the ball of dough out onto a well-floured surface and knead for 6 to 8 minutes, until dough is smooth and elastic. After kneading, cover dough with a clean linen cloth and let rest for 10 minutes.

As dough rests, prepare your baking sheets. Lightly grease two baking sheets or cover them with parchment paper. Sprinkle with cornmeal or corn flour.

Shape the dough by first dividing the dough into two even pieces, then shape each piece into a round or oval shape. Place the loaves on the prepared pans and slash the tops diagonally using a sharp, flat-bladed knife or bread lame. Cover with a clean, damp towel or oiled plastic wrap and let rise in a warm place until nearly doubled in size.

After rising, just before baking, beat the egg white lightly with a fork and brush lightly all over the loaves.

Bake loaves at 375° for 25-35 minutes.

**To use to make garlic bread, prepare and bake the Italian bread. Let bread cool for 20-30 minutes or store the bread until ready to make the garlic bread.

Melt ¼ cup butter per loaf and add one or two minced garlic cloves (if using garlic powder or minced garlic, substitute 1 teaspoon per clove of fresh garlic). Sprinkle in some parsley if desired, and/or any other herbs you like.

Cut the prepared loaf in half lengthwise. Brush each half with the garlic and butter mixture. Sprinkle with grated or shredded cheese, if desired. Bake at 375°F for 10 minutes, buttered-side up, until butter starts to just slightly brown and the bread starts to crisp. You may also heat under a broiler (about 5 minutes) but do keep a close eye to prevent over-browning.

SIMPLE, SWEET, & SAVORY BUNS & ROLLS

CLASSIC WHITE DINNER ROLLS

Our basic white bread recipe is highly versatile and makes a very good dinner roll. If you're looking for something a little richer and more robust in a dinner roll, though, try this one on for size. With added egg and butter, it's that much more well-rounded, making it a hearty and delicious addition to any meal.

- 5 C all-purpose flour
- 3 TBSP sugar
- ½ tsp salt
- 4 tsp instant yeast
- 1 ½ C very warm water (about 120°F)
- ¼ C butter, melted
- 1 large egg, lightly beaten

In a large mixing bowl, combine the flour, sugar, salt, and instant yeast. Stir through to combine.

Add the water and melted butter, and then the egg. Mix through until thoroughly combined and dough comes together as a ball.

Turn the dough out onto a well-floured surface and knead for 6 to 8 minutes, until smooth and elastic. Cover dough with a clean linen cloth and let rest for 10 minutes.

While the dough rests, prepare your baking pans. Grease two 9x13 pans. After the dough has rested for 10 minutes, form the dough into balls about 1 ½ inches in size and place the balls in the prepared pans (3 balls across, 4 down the length of the pan, 12 rolls per pan – they will double in size and lightly rise together; this batch should make about 24 rolls, fewer if the balls are larger). Cover the pans of rolls with a clean, damp towel or oiled plastic wrap and let rise in a warm place until doubled.

Bake at 350° for 20 to 25 minutes, until nicely browned. If desired, brush tops with melted butter while hot.

CORNMEAL ROLLS

These rolls turn the interest factor up a notch and deliver an option outside the norm of white or wheat. Soft like white bread but with a touch of corn flavor and the essence of cornbread, this is a tasty soft dinner roll that pairs well with any meal, but especially soups and chili. It does require a few more steps, but they're well worth that small added effort.

- 1 ⅔ C milk
- ⅔ C cornmeal
- ⅔ C sugar
- ½ C butter
- 1 tsp salt
- ¼ C warm water
- 4 to 6 C all-purpose flour
- 2 TBSP instant yeast
- 2 eggs, lightly beaten

Heat the milk in a small saucepan on the stovetop, just until it comes to a simmer. Next, add in the cornmeal, sugar, butter, and salt. Cook until slightly thickened. Add the warm water to the mixture and stir through. Set aside and let the mixture cool until it is a little under 120°F.

Begin the next steps when the cornmeal mixture has cooled to around 120° or just below. In a large mixing bowl, add 4 cups of all-purpose flour and the yeast. Stir through to distribute. Lightly beat the eggs and then add them to the flour and yeast. Next, add the cooked cornmeal mixture into the dry ingredients. Stir with a heavy spoon until smooth. At this point, the dough may be very wet; if it is, add additional flour in ½ cup increments, mixing after each addition, until a slightly sticky but smooth and elastic dough is formed. (*Moisture absorption in this recipe can be highly variable, owing to the grind, type, or brand of cornmeal used; your dough may or may not require additional flour.)

Once the dough has come together, turn it out onto a well-floured surface. Knead the dough for about 6 minutes. As you knead the dough, you may find that it needs a bit more flour worked into it to make it workable. Work in flour until you have a fairly smooth and elastic dough, but don't overdo it or the rolls become dense and lose flavor. Let the dough stay just a little on the "wetter" side of normal; as the dough rests in the next step, the cornmeal will continue to absorb some of this extra moisture.

After kneading, cover the dough with a clean linen cloth and let it rest for 10 minutes. As it rests, prepare your baking pans. Grease a cookie sheet or two 9x13 cake pans or line with parchment paper.

Once the dough has rested, use floured hands to shape the rolls. Divide the dough into about 18 even balls and lightly shape, then place on the pan, leaving room for rising (to about double; place a bit closer for pull-apart rolls and let them rise into each other). Cover pans with a damp towel or oiled/sprayed plastic wrap and let rise in a warm, draft-free place until doubled, usually about one-half hour to 45 minutes.

Bake in a 350°F oven for 20 to 25 minutes, until lightly browned. Brush with butter immediately after removing from oven. Best served warm.

CHALLAH-STYLE KNOTTED ROLLS

These single-serve Challah-styled knots lend the serving ease of dinner rolls and the flavor of a traditional bread made simpler with this instant yeast bread baking method. The recipe makes two dozen, plenty for a family dinner or crowd, but the knots also freeze well once baked. If two dozen is a bit more for your immediate needs, throw some in the freezer or cut the recipe measurements in half. (Incidentally, if you prefer a loaf, prepare the recipe and form into a braided Challah-style bread instead. Increase baking time as needed.)

- 7 C all-purpose flour
- 2 ½ TBSP instant yeast
- 2 tsp sugar
- 4 tsp salt
- ½ C honey
- ½ C vegetable oil
- 8 egg yolks
- 2 C very warm water

For the egg wash:

- 2 TBSP water

- **2 eggs**

In a large mixing bowl, combine the flour, instant yeast, sugar, and salt and stir through to evenly distribute.

In a separate small mixing bowl or large liquid measuring cup, combine the honey, the oil, and the egg yolks. Lightly beat the mixture with a fork.

Add the honey mixture to the dry ingredients and then add in the warm water. Stir until combined and dough comes together as a ball.

Turn the dough out onto a well-floured surface. Knead the dough for 8 to 10 minutes. Expect the dough to be somewhat sticky and work in additional flour as you knead the dough (in ¼ cup increments) until a smooth, elastic, and only slightly sticky dough is formed.

Cover the dough with a clean linen cloth and let rest for 10 minutes.

After the dough has rested, prepare your pans. Use a large cookie sheet (two if necessary) or two 9x13 rectangular pans. Grease the pan(s) or line with parchment paper.

Shape the rolls into knots. First, divide the dough into about 24 even balls (less if you prefer larger knots). On a lightly floured surface, roll each ball out into a long "snake-like" rope, about 8 to 10 inches long. Tie a loose knot with the rope and tuck the ends under. Transfer to the prepared pan (using a flat spatula is helpful to maintain the rolls' shapes). After you have shaped all the rolls, cover with oiled plastic wrap or a damp linen towel, place in a warm, draft-free spot and let rise until doubled, about half an hour.

Just before baking, prepare the egg wash by combining the eggs and water and whisking until smooth. Use a pastry brush and brush the wash all over the knots. Be sure to cover the exposed sides to lend a nice, all-over shine.

Bake knots at 350°F for about 20 minutes (longer if needed for larger knots), until tops are nicely browned.

CIABATTA ROLLS

If you like those light and airy, chewy, Italian-style sandwich rolls, you will love this pared-down version of them. Because we let them rise to a larger-than-normal degree, the overall time investment is a bit more, but the active prep time really is not, and the results are well worth the slightly extended wait. Incidentally, if you'd like a ciabatta-style loaf, simply cut to loaf size and shape when cutting the dough.

- 3 ¼ C all-purpose flour
- 2 tsp instant yeast
- 2 tsp salt
- 1 ½ tsp sugar
- 1 ⅔ C cool to lukewarm water (about 85°F)
- 5 TBSP olive oil
- *Optional for flavored rolls: ⅛ C fresh or 1 TBSP dried herbs and/or ¼ C grated or shredded cheese
- Extra olive oil for pan and for brushing baked rolls

In a large mixing bowl, combine the flour, instant yeast, salt, and sugar, and mix through to combine (if incorporating herbs, add them with the dry ingredients). Add the water and olive oil all at once. Stir with a sturdy mixing spoon until combined and dough starts to come together as a ball.

Turn the dough out onto a floured surface and knead for 6 to 8 minutes, until dough is smooth and elastic. Cover the dough with a clean linen cloth and let rest for 10 minutes.

Once dough has rested, cut and split the dough into two equal portions. Oil two 9 x 13 baking pans with olive oil (oil well but avoid making puddles of oil). Place a portion of dough into each oiled pan. Lightly oil your fingers and gently stretch the dough so that it covers the bottom of the pans, but do not tear the dough. Oil or spray sheets of plastic wrap and cover the pans of dough. Let dough rise in a warm, draft-free place until it reaches to the top of the pan (this will be more than the normal doubled size). rising time may take significantly longer than most bread doughs, as much as 1 ½ hours or more.

When dough has risen, oil two large baking or cookie sheets with olive oil. Invert the pan of dough onto the oiled baking sheet. Tap the dough pan to help release the ciabatta dough. Using a large, sharp knife, cut each pan of dough into 6 equal squares. Push squares apart so that they do not rise into each other during baking. Leave 2 to 3 inches between rolls. Cover pans again with well-oiled/sprayed plastic wrap and let rise again, about 20 to 30 minutes more (rolls should rise by about another 50%). If you are flavoring with grated or shredded cheese, sprinkle it over the tops of the rolls before this final rise.

Preheat your oven to 450°F. Bake rolls for 20 to 25 minutes or until golden brown. Brush tops with olive oil when removed from oven and cool completely before using.

*Note that this recipe makes one dozen rolls and these rolls freeze well. If you plan to freeze or reheat rolls prior to use, it is best to bake them through, but on the light side, until they are just very lightly beginning to brown. Heat in a 325°F oven for 10 to 15 minutes to reheat before using. May be heated from frozen.

HEARTY OATMEAL DINNER ROLLS

This recipe varies only slightly from others in this book. To start, we combine the wet ingredients with the oats, which allows the oats the time they need to absorb good moisture so that the rolls are soft when finished. Worth noting, the instruction to use boiling water is not a misprint – the heat helps to pre-cook the oats; with the addition of cold water in later steps, by the time the yeast is introduced, the oats will have cooled and disbursed the excess heat so as not to cause a problem for the yeast. Still utilizing instant yeast, the rest of the recipe will look familiar and will save you a lot of time, too. It's all very much worthwhile for this flavorful dinner roll with a whole-grain boost.

- 1 ½ C boiling water
- 2 TBSP oil (or melted butter)
- 2 tsp salt
- 1 C rolled or "Old-fashioned" oats
- ¾ C cold water
- 5 ½ C all-purpose flour, divided
- ¼ C brown sugar
- 2 ½ tsp instant yeast
- ¼ C molasses

Measure out 2 cups of the boiling water and add the oil (or butter) and salt to the water. Measure the oats into a large mixing bowl, and then carefully add the boiling water mixture to it. Stir, being careful not to splash the very hot liquid, until combined. Let sit for 3 minutes.

Next, pour in the cold water and stir until combined. Let the mixture sit and cool for 5 minutes, then proceed.

To the oat mixture, add 2 cups of the flour, the sugar, and instant yeast. Stir to distribute. Add the molasses and stir to distribute once more. Now stir in the remaining flour, one cup at a time, until all is combined and evenly mixed.

Turn the dough out onto a well-floured surface and knead for 6 minutes, then let dough rest for 10 minutes.

After the dough has rested, rub your hands with butter to keep this slightly sticky dough from sticking as you work. Shape the dough into evenly-sized rolls. The dough should yield about 24 dinner rolls. Place the formed rolls onto a greased or parchment-lined cookie sheet and cover. Let rolls rise until doubled in size (about 45 minutes) and bake at 350°F for 20-24 minutes. Brush hot rolls with melted butter immediately after removing from oven.

FAST & EASY HERB & CHEESE GARLIC KNOTS

Herbs and cheese, garlic and butter, soft knots of bread, dipped in all of it. The perfect companion for a nice Italian dinner, or just about anything else. Double the batch, there's never enough. And you WILL be looking for the leftovers!

- 1 C milk
- 4 TBSP butter
- 1 TBSP honey (for more savory) or sugar
- 3 ½ C flour
- ½ tsp salt
- 2 TBSP instant yeast
- 1 beaten egg

Garlic butter for glazing:

- 4 TBSP melted butter
- 4 TBSP grated Parmesan or Romano Cheese (finely grated cheese will work better for this recipe)
- 2 cloves garlic, minced (or about 1 tsp minced garlic) – more to taste as desired

- ¼ tsp garlic powder (more to taste)
- ½ tsp Italian Seasoning

In the microwave or on your stovetop, heat milk to scalding (about 120°F). Add the first 4 tablespoons of melted butter. Add the honey (or sugar) to the milk now. Stir to combine. Set aside.

In a large bowl, mix together the flour, salt, instant yeast. Add the beaten egg to the dry mixture, and then add the milk mixture. Stir well to combine.

Turn the dough out onto a well-floured surface and knead the dough for 6 to 8 minutes, until dough is smooth and elastic. If necessary, add more flour in small amounts to bring the dough to the desired consistency as you knead (one or two tablespoons at a time). Do note that this dough should be a softer dough. Make it only firm enough to be workable; it will be a little bit tacky.

After kneading, cover the dough with a clean linen towel and let it rest for just 3 to 5 minutes, then start dividing and working it into knots. Divide the dough into 12 even balls and shape into knots (lightly oil or flour hands as needed). To make the knots, roll each ball into a long rope, then "tie" a loose single knot; tuck the ends under or let them hang – whatever you prefer. Place the knots on a lightly greased or parchment-lined baking sheet (knots should not touch and do leave room for rising without touching). Cover knots with a damp linen cloth or oiled plastic wrap and let rise for 15 minutes. Preheat oven to 400°F while knots are resting.

Bake in 400°F oven 10 to 12 minutes, until nicely browned. Do not let them over-darken.

While the knots bake, prepare the garlic butter and herb mixture. Melt the butter, then add the remaining topping ingredients to the butter. Whisk with a fork to distribute herbs, cheese, and garlic. Set aside and keep warm until ready to use. Whisk again just before using.

When knots are done baking, let cool for a few minutes until you can comfortably handle them. Dip the knots individually, one at a time, in the garlic-butter mixture. Coat all around. Set back on tray and let cool until topping is firm.

Delicious enjoyed warm but also tasty when cooled, these knots also reheat well. To reheat, warm for 5 to 10 minutes in a warm oven, or warm for about 30 seconds in a microwave.

ROLL-STYLE GARLIC DINNER ROLLS

Any fan of garlic bread will absolutely love these rolls. Rolled up and cut cinnamon-roll style, they pack a ton of garlicky goodness in every bite. These rolls present well and also offer the added benefit of being simpler to serve to a crowd. An awful lot going for these delicious dinner buns!

- 1 ½ C milk (heated to scalding and then cooled to very warm – about 110-120°F)
- 6 TBSP melted butter
- 4 C flour
- 2 tsp salt
- 1/3 C sugar
- 2 ¼ tsp (or 1 envelope) instant yeast

Garlic-Butter Filling:

- ½ C softened, workable butter
- 2-3 cloves minced garlic
- 1/4 C freshly-chopped parsley (⅛ C if using dried)
- salt and pepper to taste

In your microwave or on the stovetop, heat the milk to scalding and then cool to at least 120°. Add the melted butter and set aside.

In a large mixing bowl, place the flour, salt, sugar, and yeast together and stir to mix through.

Pour in the milk and butter mixture and stir to combine until mixture comes together in a ball.

Turn the dough out onto a well-floured surface and knead for 6 to 8 minutes. If dough is too wet and sticky, work in additional flour a couple of tablespoons at a time (keeping in mind that this dough should be a little wetter and stickier than typical bread dough). Cover with a clean linen towel or plastic wrap and let dough rest for 10 minutes.

While dough rests, prepare the garlic-butter filling by working all ingredients into the soft butter and mixing until garlic and herbs are uniformly distributed.

After the dough has rested, turn the dough out onto a floured surface and pat or roll the dough into a flat rectangle about 10 x 15 inches in size. Spread the garlic-butter mixture evenly over the entire surface of the dough.

Now shape the dough into a large roll and then cut. Starting with the long side, roll the dough cinnamon roll-style. Lightly pinch the seam and place the seam on the bottom of the roll. Cut the roll into even slices using a sharp, flat knife or pastry cutter. Slices should be about 1 ½ inches thick. Yield should be about one dozen. Lay the slices out on a parchment-lined or lightly greased baking sheet. Set the rolls close but not touching, leaving room for the rolls to rise and touch as they rise. Cover the rolls with a damp cloth or oiled plastic wrap and allow to rise in a warm, draft-free place until doubled (usually about 45 minutes).

Bake at 375° for 15 to 20 minutes, until golden brown on top.

Tip: if you find that your garlic rolls over-brown before the middles are cooked through, tent the pan with aluminum foil during baking. Remove foil for the last 5 minutes of baking.

PULL-APART GARLIC KNOT 'MONKEY' BREAD

A little extra time and effort in shaping this mountain of pull-apart knots will not go unappreciated. And the reward? So very worth the effort. (Think "monkey" bread for garlic knots). Soft, cheesy, garlicky goodness!

- 3 ½ C all-purpose flour
- 2 tsp salt
- 1 tsp sugar
- 2 tsp instant yeast
- 1 ⅓ C very warm water (110-120°)
- 2 TBSP olive oil

Garlic Butter:

- ½ C butter, melted
- 6 cloves finely minced garlic
- 2 TBSP parsley

Cheese Mixture:

- ¼ C (more to taste if desired) parmesan cheese, grated

- ½ C (more to taste if desired) mozzarella cheese, shredded

In a large mixing bowl, combine the flour, salt, sugar, and instant yeast; stir through to distribute and then add olive oil and warm water all together. Mix well with a sturdy spoon until ingredients are thoroughly combined and dough comes together into a large ball.

Turn dough out onto a well-floured surface and knead for 6 to 8 minutes. Cover the dough with a clean linen cloth or sprayed plastic wrap and let dough rest for 10 minutes.

While you wait, prepare the garlic butter in one bowl and set aside, and then prepare the cheese mixture in a separate bowl and set that aside until ready to use.

To prepare garlic butter: Melt the butter. Add minced garlic to the melted butter, and then the parsley. Stir through to distribute and combine. Set aside and let flavors blend until ready to use. Keep warm and melted (but mixture can be reheated if necessary).

To prepare cheese mixture: combine mozzarella and parmesan together in a bowl, stir through to evenly combine, and set aside until ready to use.

After the dough has rested, divide the dough into even pieces. Shape pieces into balls. Balls should be about the size of golf balls and the dough should yield about 20 golf ball-sized portions.

To make the knots, roll the balls on your floured surface until they form a long rope, and then tie each rope into a single knot shape: For each knot, roll the ball into a rope and then "tie" into a knot shape. Dip each knot in the garlic butter mixture as you work. Be sure to coat the entire surface.

Assemble the knots into the pull-apart mound as you go. Assemble as follows into a springform pan (a Bundt pan or high-sided 8- or 9-inch round pan can also be used if you do not have a springform pan, but springform pans are easiest to work with).

To form the mound:

- Place the first half of the shaped, dipped knots on the bottom of the springform pan so that they almost touch.
- After placing the first layer, sprinkle half of the cheese mixture over the layer of knots.
- Shape and dip the remaining dough into knots and stack them on top of the first knot/cheese layer.
- Sprinkle the remaining cheese mixture over the top of the knots.

After shaping, cover the pan with sprayed or oiled plastic wrap or a damp linen towel. Set in a warm, draft-free place and let rise until about doubled (about half an hour, depending on the temperature and conditions in your kitchen).

Once risen, bake the pull-apart at 350°F for 35-40 minutes or until golden brown. (If bread darkens too quickly before the center bakes through, the mound can be tented with foil, but first spray the foil with cooking spray or coat with oil and try not to let the foil touch the bread and cheese; remove foil in the last 10 minutes to allow for browning.)

STUFFED GARLIC CHEESY BUNS

You can use any favorite cheese in this recipe to truly personalize it to your own taste. Here, we've used a combination of cheddar and mozzarella with parmesan. The cheddar gives it that delicious, tell-tale flavor while the mozzarella brings a bit of tang and gooey, stretchy, melty goodness, topped off with parmesan for an added flavor boost. Since you can never go wrong with garlic and cheese, these buns pair with practically any dish you'd think to serve them with.

- 3 C all-purpose flour
- 2 TBSP sugar
- 2 tsp salt
- 2 tsp garlic powder (optional but recommended)
- 2 TBSP instant yeast
- ¼ C olive oil
- ¼ C butter, melted
- 1 cup very warm water (about 110-120°)

For the filling:

- 1 C (8 Oz.) mozzarella, cut into cubes (about ½-¾ inch)

For the topping:

- ½ C (4 Oz.) shredded cheddar cheese
- ¼ C grated parmesan cheese

In a large mixing bowl, combine the flour, sugar, salt, and garlic powder (if using), and the instant yeast. Stir through to distribute, then add the olive oil and melted butter all together. Stir through once more to combine ingredients.

Pour in the warm water and stir with a sturdy spoon until ingredients are mixed through and dough comes together as a ball.

Turn the dough out onto a well-floured surface and knead for 6 to 8 minutes. After kneading, cover with a clean linen cloth or oiled/sprayed plastic wrap and let rest for 10 minutes.

After the dough has rested, use a large kitchen knife or bench scraper and divide the dough into about 20 balls of even size. (If you prefer a larger-sized bun, make fewer, larger pieces and use two cubes of cheese in each. Baking time may need to be adjusted). Flatten each ball slightly with the palm of your hand and place a cube of the mozzarella in the center of each ball. Fold the dough over and pinch the seam well to close. Roll lightly to reshape into a ball. Place buns, seam-side down, onto a greased or parchment paper-lined baking sheet.

After you have shaped and placed all of the buns on the baking sheet, sprinkle the tops with the parmesan cheese and then the shredded cheddar. Cover the buns with a damp linen cloth or an oiled/sprayed piece of plastic wrap and let rise in a warm, draft-free place until about doubled.

Bake buns at 375°F for 14-16 minutes. Buns should be golden brown and the cheese should be melted and bubbly on the top. Remove from oven when done and, if desired, brush tops with melted butter. Best served warm.

QUICK AND EASY CROISSANTS

Traditional, "real" croissants are a true labor of love. They require a multi-step process of rolling, buttering, cooling, and repeating multiple times to "laminate" them. The process can literally extend into days. This recipe, however, is far more simplified. The result is a croissant very close to the real deal, but without a days-long investment. Use them any way you would use croissants, including as a replacement in recipes that call for preservative-laden frozen or refrigerator croissant doughs. Additionally, these croissants make an excellent base for any kind of fillings, from sweet chocolate to savory meats and cheeses.

- 1 ¼ C warm milk (about 120°)
- 3 ⅓ C all-purpose flour (additional as needed)
- 1 C cold butter, cut into chunks
- 1 TBSP sugar
- ½ tsp salt
- 2 ¼ tsp (equal to 1 envelope) instant yeast
- 2 eggs, separated – reserve both whites and yolks for use
- 1 egg white (for brushing)

In a microwave or on your stovetop, heat the milk to between 120° and 130°. Set aside.

In a large mixing bowl, combine the flour and chunks of butter. Cut in the butter chunks, using a pastry blender or your hands, and work the butter into the flour until the butter is about the size of peas. Butter should be evenly distributed throughout.

Next, add the sugar, salt, and yeast, and mix through to combine. Add the 2 egg yolks and stir (but not the whites – cover and refrigerate them for later use). Pour in the hot milk and stir with a sturdy spoon until the ingredients are well combined and the dough starts to come together as a ball. Do not knead this dough at this time.

Cover the bowl and place in the refrigerator to cool. Cool for at least two hours and be sure the dough has cooled completely before trying to work it. Dough may be left to cool for several hours, if more convenient.

When dough is cold, form the croissants. First, line a baking sheet with parchment paper or lightly grease it. Turn the cold dough out onto a lightly floured surface and knead it a few times, just until it is smooth and workable. Try not to let the dough get too warm. Divide the dough into three balls. Keep the extra balls cold while you work the others (return resting dough to refrigerator if necessary).

Roll each ball into a circle about 16-18 inches round. Using a pastry or pizza cutter or a large, flat-bladed knife, cut the circle into 8 or 10 even wedges (depending on how large you want your croissants to be and how many you want to yield; you can do fewer, too, but adjust baking time for smaller or larger rolls).

Starting with the long side of the wedges, roll each piece toward the small point and then bend slightly to form a crescent shape. Tuck the point to the underside of the crescent and place on the prepared baking sheet with enough space for rising without touching. [**Note: if you want to stuff your croissants, lay fillers on croissants prior to rolling. Leave room around the edges to seal in fillers. Gently press as you roll croissants to hold the fillers in place. You can stuff with baking chips, nuts, etc., or sliced and cut deli meat, cubed meats and cheeses, shredded cheese...]

After all of the rolls are formed, cover the pan with a damp linen towel or oiled/sprayed plastic wrap and let rise in a warm, draft-free place until about doubled in size. Since the dough is cold to start, rising time may take a little longer than other rolls; depending on kitchen conditions, average rising time is 45 to 60 minutes.

When rolls are ready to bake, beat the reserved egg whites and lightly brush the rolls with the beaten egg whites. Bake croissants at 375°F for 20-22 minutes or until done (reduce the time for smaller rolls; increase slightly for large croissants). Croissants should be a nice, golden brown. Let cool slightly before serving.

Croissants are best enjoyed warm but may also be enjoyed cold as a sandwich roll. To prep ahead for future use, bake through as instructed, cool, and then, if desired, warm for about 10 minutes in a low oven.

BUTTER-BABY CRESCENT ROLLS

Buttery and delicious, these crescent rolls are wonderful as dinner rolls, breakfast rolls, brunch buddies, or any time you might want something a little stepped-up without too much fuss. Additionally, they make a great clean, homemade option for recipes calling for pre-made or refrigerator crescent rolls. They are also ideal for filling with things like chocolate chips or baking chips, meats, cheeses, sausages, herbs, or savories.

One thing worth noting – crescent rolls are easiest to work if the dough has a period of rest and cooling in the refrigerator after the dough is formed. This improves the texture of the finished roll but also helps to make the dough more workable and manageable as you form the rolls. It is best to plan this dough when you have a few hours to let it refrigerate before finishing. It can also be made ahead the day or night before, then quickly finished off for dinner the next day for fresh, warm, crescent rolls ready to go. If you must skip the cooling period, it can be done, but the best results will be enjoyed if you plan in that period of cooling.

- 1 C hot water
- ½ C butter (can substitute if necessary; real butter lends best result)
- 4 C all-purpose flour

- ½ C sugar
- 1 tsp salt
- 2 ¼ tsp instant yeast (equal to 1 package)
- 2 eggs, lightly beaten
- **Extra soft butter to spread on dough; about 1 stick**

Measure one cup of hot water. Cut the ½ cup butter into chunks and add to the hot water. Set aside and let butter soften. You do not need the butter to melt completely, just to soften through. Some melting is okay, but you should have some soft chunks left, too.

In a large bowl, combine the flour, sugar, salt, and yeast. Stir through to combine. Add the lightly beaten eggs and the water/butter mixture. Stir until dough comes together and begins to form a ball (dough may be sticky and loose at this point, looser than most bread doughs, and that is okay; you will add flour as you knead to make it more workable, and refrigerating will aid in manageability, too).

Turn the dough out onto a floured surface. Knead dough for six minutes. Add flour one tablespoon at a time as needed as you work to firm up the dough, but do not add more than ¼ cup flour to the dough or it will become tough. This dough will be a lighter and softer, somewhat stickier dough. After kneading, return the dough to an oiled bowl and cover. Ideally, you should refrigerate the dough to let it firm up before proceeding. A minimum of three hours is best, or you can refrigerate the dough overnight and work it the next day.

When ready to proceed, prepare your baking sheet by either lightly greasing it or by lining it with parchment paper. Turn the cold dough out onto a lightly floured surface and divide the dough in half. Keep the second half cold as you work the first ball (return it to the refrigerator if necessary).

Roll each ball into a thin circle, about ¼ inch thick. Spread butter over the entire surface of the round. Now, using a pizza or pastry cutter or sharp, flat-bladed knife, cut the round into 8 to 10 pie-shaped wedges (depending on the desired size of rolls). Work each wedge as its own roll.

Quick-Time Homemade Bread and Pastries

Starting with the long side, roll the dough toward the point and tuck the point to the bottom side of the crescent. If you are filling the crescents, spread or sprinkle fillings over the wedge just prior to filling. Place each roll on the prepared baking sheet, leaving enough room for rolls to rise to about double in size. When all crescents are prepared, cover the pan with a sprayed or oiled sheet of plastic wrap, or a damp linen towel.

Let dough rise until doubled in a warm, draft-free place. Allow for a slightly longer rising period than normal, as the dough is starting the process cold (typical rising time is 45-60 minutes).

Preheat oven to 375°F and bake rolls for 8 to 10 minutes or until golden brown and done. enjoy warm or cold, or lightly reheat to warm through.

RISE AND SHINE CINNAMON ROLLS

We'd all enjoy more warm, soft cinnamon rolls if we could just find the time. Thanks to this fast and easy recipe, now you can! Real, yeast-risen cinnamon rolls ready to wake the house and enjoy with your coffee, in just a little more than an hour.

- 1 egg plus hot water to equal 1 ½ C
- 4 ½ C all-purpose flour
- ½ C sugar
- 1 ½ tsp salt
- 1 ½ tsp instant yeast
- ⅓ C melted butter (or oil)

For the filling:

- ½ C sugar
- 3 TBSP ground cinnamon
- ½ cup softened butter

For the glaze:

- ¾ C powdered confectioner's sugar
- ¼ C milk (more if you prefer thinner glaze)
- ½ teaspoon vanilla extract

First, crack the egg into a two-cup measuring cup and then add enough hot water until the unit measures 1 ½ cups total liquid. Set aside.

In a large mixing bowl, combine the flour, sugar, salt, and instant yeast. Stir through to combine. Add the melted butter and water and egg mixture all at once. Stir with a sturdy spoon to mix through, until dough comes together as a ball.

Turn the dough out onto a floured surface and knead for about 6 to 8 minutes. After kneading, cover the dough with a clean linen cloth and let rest for 10 minutes.

While the dough rests, prepare the filling. Combine the cinnamon and ½ cup sugar and mix through to evenly distribute the ingredients. Set aside.

After the dough has rested, roll or pat the dough into a rectangle, about 12 by 24 inches long. Spread the softened butter evenly over the dough and then generously sprinkle the buttered dough with the cinnamon-sugar mixture.

Prepare a baking sheet by either lining it with parchment paper or lightly greasing it. Now form the rolls: Start with the long side and roll the dough up, jelly-roll style. End with the seam underneath and gently pinch it to keep it from unrolling. Cut the roll into one-inch slices. Place the slices on their sides on the prepared baking sheet, leaving enough room for rolls to rise to about double. Cover the rolls with a damp linen cloth or oiled/sprayed plastic wrap. Let rise in a warm, draft-free place for about 30 to 45 minutes or until doubled, then bake.

Bake in a preheated 350° oven for about 25 minutes, or until golden brown on top and baked through.

While the rolls are baking, prepare the glaze by combining the milk, vanilla, and powdered sugar, and whisking until smooth. Set aside until ready to use.

When rolls are done baking, remove from the oven and let cool for about 5 minutes. Drizzle all over with glaze. Serve warm and enjoy. (Note – to serve leftover cinnamon rolls warm, reheat for about 20 to 30 seconds in the microwave.)

NUTTY STICKY BUNS

Perfect for breakfast or brunch, these caramelly-sweet sticky nut buns are also delicious at any time of the day. Coffee, tea, dinner, or after, there's never a bad time to serve these up (preferably just a touch warm, but any way you dish them is a good way to serve them!).

- 1 egg plus hot water to equal 1 ¼ C
- 3 ½ C all-purpose flour
- ⅓ C sugar
- 1 tsp salt
- 1 ½ tsp instant yeast
- ¼ C melted butter

For the filling:

- ½ C (1 stick) softened butter
- ⅓ C sugar
- 1 TBSP cinnamon

For the topping:

- ¾ C melted butter
- ¾ C packed light brown sugar (substitute dark if preferred)
- ½ C chopped nuts (pecans or walnuts are best; may omit if preferred or substitute favorite nuts)

Crack the egg into a two-cup measuring cup. Add hot water until the total liquid volume equals 1 ¼ cups. Set aside.

In a large mixing bowl, combine the flour, sugar, salt, and instant yeast. Stir through to combine.

Add the melted butter and the hot water and egg mixture all at once. Using a sturdy spoon, stir until mixed through and dough starts to come together as a ball.

Turn dough out onto a well-floured surface and knead for 6 to 8 minutes. Cover kneaded dough with a clean linen towel and let rest for 10 minutes.

Prepare the filling and the topping while dough is resting. Combine the cinnamon and sugar and mix through until ingredients are evenly distributed. Set aside.

For the filling, combine cinnamon and sugar and mix through. Set aside until ready to use.

To make the topping, combine the brown sugar and the melted butter. Mix well. Spread the brown sugar and butter mixture evenly over the bottom of a baking sheet. Be sure the sheet has at least ½ inch sides or use two 9x13 inch cake pans and divide the topping in half, spreading the mixture evenly over the bottom of each. Now sprinkle the chopped nuts evenly over the butter and brown sugar in the bottom of the pan(s). Set aside while buns are formed.

When dough has rested, roll or gently pat the dough into a large rectangle, about 12 x 18 inches. Spread the ½ cup softened butter over the surface of the rectangle. Next, sprinkle the entire surface with the cinnamon sugar mix. Roll the dough up jelly-roll style, starting with the longest side; end with the seam towards the bottom and pinch seam lightly to hold the roll together. Cut the roll into about 18 even slices, each about 1 inch thick. Place buns on their sides in the prepared pan atop the mixture of brown sugar, butter, and nuts. Space evenly to allow room to rise, but closely enough so that the whole surface of the pan will be covered when risen and buns will just touch when they do rise. Cover the pan with a damp linen cloth or oiled/sprayed plastic wrap. Let rise in a warm, draft-free place until about doubled in size.

Bake sticky buns on the top rack of a preheated oven at 350° for 25-30 minutes. Rolls should be golden brown. watch closely towards the end of the time, as the sugars on the bottom can burn easily.

Remove buns from the oven and quickly but carefully flip the pan of buns over onto a heat-proof tray or second large baking sheet. Flip buns completely upside down when you invert them so that the bottom of the pan with the caramelized brown sugar, butter, and nuts becomes the top of the finished buns. The mixture you spread over the bottom of the pan now becomes the topping for your sticky buns.

Cool buns slightly before serving. May be served warm, cool, or gently reheated.

SWEET BITES MINI CINNAMON BUNS

Looking for a tasty but simpler alternative to cinnamon rolls? You might just love these cinnamon bun bites! Smaller and less filling than large cinnamon rolls, these bites work up quickly and make an excellent grab-n-go, brunch, or buffet treat. Even better, the addition of brown sugar into the coating lends a unique flavor, too.

- 4 C all-purpose flour
- 2 TBSP sugar
- 1 TBSP instant yeast
- 1 tsp salt
- 1 ½ C very warm water (115-120°)
- 2 TBSP oil or melted butter

For coating:

- ½ C melted butter
- ¾ C white sugar
- ¼ C packed light brown sugar
- 1 TBSP cinnamon

For the icing:

- 1 C Confectioner's powdered sugar
- 2 TBSP melted butter
- ½ tsp vanilla extract
- 2 to 3 TBSP milk

In a large mixing bowl, combine the flour, sugar, salt, and instant yeast. Stir through to combine. Add the oil and the warm water all at once. Using a sturdy spoon, stir until combined and dough starts to come together in a ball.

Turn dough out onto a well-floured surface and knead for 6 to 8 minutes. After kneading, cover the dough with a clean linen cloth and let rest for 10 minutes.

While the dough rests, prepare the coating. Combine the white and brown sugars and the cinnamon. Use a fork to mix through until ingredients are evenly distributed. In a separate bowl or saucepan, melt the butter. Cover and set aside until ready to use.

Prepare a baking pan by lightly greasing it or lining it with parchment paper.

When dough is rested, form the bites. Cut or tear the dough into evenly-sized pieces and form into balls, about one inch in size. Dip each ball into the melted butter and then roll it to coat in the cinnamon and sugar mixture. Place the balls on the prepared baking sheet, allowing space for the bites to rise without touching. Continue forming bites until all of the dough is used up. Cover with a damp linen towel or oiled/sprayed plastic wrap and let rise in a warm, draft-free place until bites have almost doubled.

When bites are nearing the end of the rising period, preheat oven to 375° and bake bites for about 12 minutes, or until done.

While the bites bake, prepare the icing. Combine the confectioner's sugar, vanilla, melted butter, and milk all together and whisk with a fork or small wire whisk until smooth. You may add more milk to reach your desired consistency if needed.

When bites are done baking, remove them from the oven, let cool for 5 minutes, then drizzle with the prepared icing.

RAISIN OAT DINNER ROLLS

Slightly sweet with the complementary flavors of oats and raisins, these versatile rolls bring some whole-grain goodness to your meal, whether it be breakfast, lunch, brunch, dinner, or just an afternoon snack. Using honey to sweeten them boosts the wholesome healthiness by eliminating refined white sugars as it enhances the flavor profile. What's more, these rolls keep well for a few days and are great for on-the-go.

- 3 ½ C all-purpose flour
- 1 C rolled oats
- ½ tsp salt
- 1 ½ tsp cinnamon
- 1 ½ TBSP instant yeast
- 1 cup raisins
- 3 TBSP melted butter
- 1 large egg
- ¼ C honey
- 1 cup very warm water

For glaze:

- **2 TBSP melted butter**
- **2 TBSP honey**

In a large mixing bowl, combine the flour, oats, salt, cinnamon, and instant yeast. Stir through to combine. Add in the raisins and stir through. Next, add the melted butter, honey, egg, and water all at once and stir to combine until dough begins to come together as a ball.

Turn dough out onto a well-floured surface. Knead for about 8 minutes. Dough may be sticky and if needed, you may add additional flour to make the dough smooth and elastic as you knead. When done kneading, cover the dough with a clean linen cloth and let rest for about 10 minutes.

Prepare a 9 x 13-inch pan by greasing or lining it with parchment paper. Once dough has rested, divide the dough and shape into balls of equal size and place on the prepared pan. Dough should yield about 18 rolls. Cover the pan with a damp cloth or oiled/sprayed plastic wrap and let rise in a warm, draft-free place until doubled.

Towards the end of rising, preheat the oven and prepare the glaze: Melt the butter and honey together and stir to combine. Just before baking the rolls, brush the tops and exposed sides of the rolls with the honey and butter mixture.

Bake rolls in a 400° oven for 15 minutes or until golden brown (watch closely near the end so that the honey-butter does not burn).

DONUTS, BAGELS, & SWEET BREAD TREATS

PLAIN YEAST DONUTS

Despite being a yeast-risen dough, these donuts require less rising time and work up quickly. Some say they freeze well (but then, you'd have to have enough left over to freeze to know!). As they are plain, these donuts make a good base for frosting, glazing, and topping; they do have just a touch of spice in the dough that sometimes competes, which you should feel free to leave out if you prefer.

- 2 C very warm milk (115-120°)
- 5 ½ C all-purpose flour
- 3 TBSP sugar
- 1 tsp salt
- ½ tsp cinnamon
- ½ tsp nutmeg
- 1 ½ TBSP instant yeast
- 2 eggs
- ⅓ C melted butter
- 1 tsp vanilla
- Oil or lard for frying

Heat the milk in a microwave or on the stovetop and set aside until ready to use.

In a large mixing bowl, combine the flour, sugar, salt, cinnamon, nutmeg, and instant yeast. Stir through to combine. Add the milk, melted butter, vanilla, and egg all together and mix well. Stir until dough starts to come together as a ball.

Turn dough out onto a floured surface and knead for about 5 minutes. You may knead in more flour if necessary to make the dough more workable.

After kneading, cover dough with a clean linen towel and let rest for 5 minutes.

After resting, turn dough out onto a floured surface. Pat or roll the dough out to about 1 inch thick. Use a donut cutter to cut into donut shapes. Flour or line a baking sheet with parchment paper and space donut cutouts on the sheet with room to rise. Cover with a damp linen cloth or floured/sprayed plastic wrap and let rise in a warm place for about 30 minutes, until nearly doubled.

About 10 minutes before dough is done rising, heat the fry oil or lard to about 390°. (For this, you may use an electric deep fryer or a large, heavy pan on your stovetop; use about 3 inches of oil or melted lard, but do NOT overfill the fryer or pot and leave at least 3 inches of space at the top to avoid overflowing when donuts are placed in the hot oil. Work carefully!)

Fry donuts for 3 to 4 minutes or until done, turning once halfway through. If desired, after frying, coat donuts in a mixture of cinnamon and sugar while still warm. If frosting or filling, cool first. Additional recipes for topping and filling options follow.

FILLINGS & FROSTINGS FOR PLAIN DONUTS

With the previous yeast donut recipe as your base, you can make a variety of donut flavors simply by adding fillings and frostings. These filling and topping ideas should give you a good start, but you should feel free to experiment and create your own, too. Play with different flavorings, or maybe add some additional toppings like nuts, sprinkles, and baking chips to your frostings and glazes.

Cinnamon-Coated Donuts

- 1 ½ C powdered confectioner's sugar (or granulated sugar if you prefer)
- 1 TBSP ground cinnamon

Combine the sugar and cinnamon and mix evenly. Coat each side of the donut in the mixture while the donuts are still warm.

Powdered Donuts

- 2 C powdered confectioner's sugar

Coat each side of warm donuts by dredging in the powdered sugar.

Glazed Donuts:

- 3 C powdered confectioner's sugar
- ½ tsp vanilla extract
- ½ C water or milk

Combine all ingredients and whisk until smooth. Cool donuts completely, then dip the donuts in the glaze and place on a cooling rack to set the glaze. Place newspaper or a baking sheet underneath the cooling rack to catch dripping glaze.

Honey-Glazed Donuts:

- 3 C powdered confectioner's sugar
- ½ cup melted butter
- ½ C hot water
- 1 TBSP honey
- 1 ½ tsp vanilla extract

Combine all ingredients and whisk until smooth. Place a set of cooling racks over newspaper or a baking sheet to catch drips. Dip cooled donuts in the glaze, turning to glaze both sides. Set on a cooling rack to set the glaze.

Chocolate Glaze

- 2 cups powdered confectioner's sugar
- ½ C semi-sweet chocolate chips
- ½ C butter
- ¼ C milk
- 1 TBSP light corn syrup
- 1 ½ tsp vanilla extract

In a saucepan, combine the milk, butter, corn syrup, and vanilla. Over medium heat, heat and stir until the butter is melted. Add the chocolate chips and reduce the heat to low. Heat and stir constantly until chocolate is completely melted. Remove from heat and add the confectioner's sugar. Whisk until combined and glaze is smooth. Place cooling racks over newspaper or a baking sheet. Dip cooled donuts in the glaze, turning to coat each side. Place on a cooling rack until glaze sets.

Jelly or Filled Donuts

- **Any flavor jelly, jam, or filling of choice**

Make the donuts as instructed but do *not* cut the hole out of the middle of the donuts. Donuts should be one whole round. Let fried donuts cool completely, then use a skewer or chopstick and pierce a hole from the side of the donut into the middle of the donut. Do not pierce through to the other side of the donut. With the end of the skewer in the center of the donut, gently move the skewer around to create a pocket of space. Fill a pastry bag fitted with a large metal tip with your filling of choice. Insert into the hole in the side and fill until the filling just starts to come out of the hole. If desired, sprinkle or coat the outside of the donut in granulated or powdered confectioner's sugar.

Crème-Filled Donuts

- **1 C marshmallow cream or fluff**
- **1 ½ C powdered confectioner's sugar**
- **¼ C softened butter**
- **2 tsp hot water**
- **½ tsp vanilla extract**

Combine all ingredients in a medium-sized bowl. Using a whisk or electric mixer, whip the ingredients until smooth and fluffy. Fill as per instructions for jelly or filled donuts.

YEAST-RAISED CHOCOLATE DONUTS

Ready to step up your homemade donut game? Adding a flavored donut to your repertoire might be just the thing – and what better to start with than chocolate? Just as easy as plain donuts, these chocolate yeast-raised donuts bring the flavor without adding to the workload. To take it even a step further, frost or glaze these donuts with the preceding chocolate glaze, or your favorite chocolate frosting recipe.

- ¾ C very warm milk (around 120°)
- 4 ½ C all-purpose flour
- ⅔ C sugar
- ½ C cocoa powder
- 2 tsp salt
- 1 ½ TBSP instant yeast
- 4 large eggs, lightly beaten
- 6 TBSP softened butter, cut into chunks
- 2 tsp vanilla extract
- Oil or lard for frying (lard preferred)

Heat the milk in a microwave or on the stovetop and set it aside. In a large bowl, combine the flour, sugar, cocoa powder, salt, and instant yeast and mix through. Next, add the milk, butter, eggs, and vanilla all at once. Using a sturdy spoon, stir until combined and dough starts to come together.

Turn dough out onto a well-floured surface. Knead for 5 to 6 minutes, working in additional flour ⅛ cup at a time as needed to make a smooth and elastic dough. Cover with a clean linen cloth and let rest for 10 minutes.

After resting, roll or pat the dough out to about ½ to ¾ inch think. Cut into donut shapes and place on a greased or parchment-lined baking sheet. Space to allow room for rising. Cover cut donuts with a damp linen cloth or oiled/sprayed plastic wrap and let rise in a warm, draft-free place until about doubled.

Towards the end of the rising time, heat about 3 inches of fry oil or lard in a deep fryer, large Dutch oven, or heavy-bottomed pot; make sure there are 3 inches of space at the top of the pot so that oil does not overflow the pot. Working carefully, fry the donut for 3 to 4 minutes or until done, turning once halfway through. Drain on a cooling rack placed over paper towels. If glazing or frosting, cool completely beforehand.

PLAIN BAGELS

Love bagels? Then you will love this recipe, which is among the easiest homemade bagels you will ever make. They forfeit none of the flavor or texture you find elsewhere but do give up the expense and preservatives. What's more, these bagels freeze very well, so it's always a good idea to double up on your batches when baking to have some on hand for busy mornings.

- 6 C all-purpose flour
- 3 TBSP sugar (or honey)
- 1 TBSP instant yeast
- 2 TSP salt
- 2 C very warm water (115-120)

For the glaze:

- 2 eggs, beaten

In a large bowl, combine the flour, sugar, salt, and instant yeast. Mix through to combine. Add the water and stir until the dough starts to come together in a ball.

Turn the dough out onto a well-floured surface and knead for 6 to 8 minutes. When done, cover the dough with a clean linen cloth and let rest for 10 minutes.

When dough has rested, shape the bagels. Divide the dough into evenly-sized pieces. Dough should yield about 16 bagels of regular size, or you can make bagels smaller or larger, but you may need to adjust the baking time slightly. To shape, roll each piece into a ball, then, using your thumbs, gently pull and tear the centers to make the center hole. Center hole should be about one inch in size.

Grease a baking sheet and place each formed bagel on the sheet. Leave enough room for the bagels to rise to about double in size without touching. When all bagels are formed, cover the pan with a damp towel or sprayed/oiled plastic wrap and let rise in a warm, draft-free place until doubled.

Towards the end of the rising period, bring 4 quarts of water to a boil. Add 4 tablespoons sugar or honey to the boiling water.

Try not to let the bagels over-rise. If you feel the bagels are rising too quickly before boiling, place the baking sheet(s) in the refrigerator while you work through the batch.

Working three or four bagels at a time (whatever will fit in your pot without overcrowding), simmer each bagel for about 3 minutes; turn once during simmering. Remove the bagels with a slotted spoon to drain the water and then place them back on the greased baking sheet. Brush simmered bagels with the beaten egg to glaze them prior to baking. If you would like to add toppings (such as sesame seeds, poppy seeds, dried onion or garlic, herbs, cheese, etc.) sprinkle it on the bagels over the egg wash before you bake them.

Bake bagels in a preheated 400° oven for 20-25 minutes or until they are a light golden brown.

BAGEL SEASONINGS & TOPPINGS

As mentioned, you can easily turn your basic plain bagels into flavored bagels with the addition of toppings and seasonings. For herbs and seasonings in the bagels, simply work into the dough by adding your desired herbs, spices, or cheeses into the dry ingredients in the beginning. For toppings, sprinkle over the egg wash just prior to baking. What follows here are some suggestions for seasoning additions and bagel toppings to boost your bagel game.

- **Sesame seeds**
- **Chia seeds**
- **Cracked wheat or wheat flakes**
- **Flax seeds**
- **Dried onion flakes or onion soup mix**

(Add ½ C dried onion flakes or soup mix to dough with the dry ingredients for more onion flavor, or use as topping instead)

- **Poppy seeds**
- **Poppy seeds and sea salt**

(¼ C poppy seeds and 1 TBSP sea salt combined)

- Caraway seeds
- Celery seed
- Oats and/or grains

(Rolled oats or multi-grain cereal mixes work well)

- Toasted nuts, any type

(Chopped walnuts, pecans, hazelnuts, almonds, or a mix of nuts are all good choices. Nuts can also be mixed into the bagel dough with the dry ingredients, about ½ C.)

- Fresh, frozen, or dehydrated berries, such as blueberries, raisins, or cranberries (1 C)
- Spices such as cinnamon (or a combination of spice and berry or nuts, such as cinnamon and raisins – 1 ½ tsp is a good measure for most spices)
- Cinnamon sugar for topping (or cinnamon and brown sugar for deeper flavor)
- Herbs of choice, such as thyme, basil, oregano, rosemary, Herbs de Provence, fennel (herbs combined with cheese additions are a delicious choice! Mix into dry ingredients.)
- Chopped sun-dried tomatoes (particularly good with added basil and/or cheese)

For flavor additions in the dough itself, a good general rule of thumb is one half cup dry herbs or seasonings per batch of dough (reduce to ⅓ or ¼ if you feel the flavor would be too strong). For cheeses, one half to one cup shredded or grated cheese of choice. If adding grains like oats or multi-grains, you may need to slightly increase the water in the dough if the dough appears to be too dry. Add water one tablespoon at a time until a workable consistency is reached (not too dry or too wet and sticky).

To top your bagels, you may sprinkle the topping over the egg wash or you may also brush the bagels with the egg wash, place the topping in a bowl and then dip the tops of the bagels into the topping.

TRADITIONAL EGG BAGELS

Boost flavor, protein, and nutrition with these traditionally-styled egg bagels. Great for toppings or additions, any of the previous flavoring options would be equally good with this hearty bagel.

- 6 C flour
- 3 TBSP sugar
- 1 TBSP salt
- 2 ½ tsp instant yeast
- 2 C very warm water
- 2 eggs, lightly beaten

For glazing:

- 2 egg yolks, beaten

In a large mixing bowl, combine the flour, sugar, salt, and instant yeast. Stir through to combine. Add the 2 beaten eggs and the warm water, then stir until combined and dough starts to come together in a ball.

Turn dough out onto a floured surface and knead for 6 to 8 minutes, until dough is smooth and elastic.

Cover dough with a clean linen cloth and let rest for 10 minutes.

Grease a baking sheet and shape the bagels after the dough has rested. Divide the dough into evenly-sized pieces (about 18 regularly-sized bagels – may make larger or smaller but may need to adjust baking time slightly). Roll each piece into a ball. Using your thumbs, make a one-inch hole in the center of each bagel by gently poking and pulling the center. Place each bagel on the greased baking sheet, leaving enough room for the bagels to rise without touching. When all bagels are formed, cover with a damp linen towel or oiled/sprayed plastic wrap and let rise in a warm, draft-free place until almost doubled.

When bagels are nearing double in size, begin heating the water for boiling. Bring 4 quarts of water to a boil in a large, six-quart pot or Dutch oven. Add 2 tablespoons sugar or honey. If you feel the bagels are rising too quickly as you prepare the water and boil them, place in the refrigerator to slow rising as you work through the batch.

Work 3 or 4 bagels at a time (only what will fit in your pot in a single layer), and simmer the bagels for about 3 minutes, turning once. Use a slotted spoon to remove the bagels from the water and place them back on the greased baking sheet. Brush the boiled bagels with the beaten egg yolks just before baking.

Bake in a preheated 400° oven for 20-25 minutes, or until lightly golden brown.

HONEY WHEAT BAGELS

With 50% whole wheat in the mix, this bagel recipe provides more of the high-fiber, healthy whole grains our diets call for. All-purpose white flour helps to lend rise and soft texture. Still, if you are aiming for a completely whole-grain bagel, you can either replace the measure of all-purpose flour with white whole wheat flour or with a total measure of 5 cups whole wheat flour. White whole wheat will not give you quite the rise and softness of all-purpose white but is close. All whole wheat will also result in a somewhat denser, less loftily-rising dough (which might also require adding a little more liquid when you mix), but does provide you with very good whole grains in your morning bagel. It can also be helpful to add 2 to 3 tablespoons of Vital Wheat Gluten (found in the baking aisle, helps to increase loft and texture and can be added to any bread recipe for additional softness, but can be particularly helpful in whole-grain recipes). No matter what flour or mixture you decide on, the honey in this recipe makes for a delicious compliment and you will enjoy starting your day with these homemade bagels.

- 2 C very warm water (115-120°)
- 3 TBSP honey
- 2 ¾ C all-purpose flour

- 2 C whole wheat flour
- ½ C wheat germ
- 1 ½ TBSP instant yeast
- 1 TBSP salt
- Additional water plus ¼ C honey for boiling

For the egg wash:

- 1 TBSP water
- 1 egg

Measure the water and add the honey to the warm water. Set aside until ready to use.

In a large mixing bowl, combine the flours, wheat germ, instant yeast, and salt. Stir through to combine. Add the honey and water mixture all at once. Stir to combine until dough starts to come together as a ball.

Turn dough out onto a well-floured surface. Knead for 6 to 8 minutes, until dough is smooth and elastic. Cover with a clean linen cloth and let rest for 15 minutes.

After dough has rested, divide the dough into evenly-sized balls (yields about 16 to 18 regular size bagels). You may make bagels larger or smaller but may need to slightly adjust the baking time.

Grease a baking sheet. Roll each bagel into a ball and use thumbs to make a one-inch hole in the center, then gently pull the bagels into shape. Place shaped bagels on the greased sheet, spaced so that the bagels can rise to about double in size without touching. Cover the bagels with a damp linen towel or oiled/sprayed plastic wrap and let rise in a warm, draft-free place until about doubled.

When bagels are near the end of rising, heat the water for boiling the bagels. Use a large pot (at least 6 quarts) and bring 4 quarts of water and ¼ cup honey to a boil. When bagels have risen, work a few bagels at a time and simmer each bagel for about 3 minutes, turning once. Remove with a slotted spoon and place back on the greased baking sheet.

Brush bagels with egg wash prior to baking: Whisk together the water and egg and then brush the boiled bagels with the wash.

Preheat oven to 400° and bake bagels for 20-25 minutes, until nicely browned.

ENGLISH MUFFIN BREAD

Few yeast breads are easier to prepare than English muffin bread. Risen but not kneaded, you are just a few steps and a little time away from this delicious morning treat, which delivers the taste and texture of homemade English muffins without the commitment. (Best yet, this recipe makes two loaves, so there's more to enjoy or one to pop in the freezer for the next time!)

- 2 C milk
- ½ C water
- 6 C all-purpose flour
- 1 TBSP sugar
- 2 tsp salt
- ¼ tsp baking soda
- 1 TBSP instant yeast
- **Cornmeal (for the pan)**

Heat the milk and water together to about 120°, then set aside until ready to use.

In a large mixing bowl, combine the flour, sugar, salt, baking soda, and yeast and stir to mix through. Pour in the heated milk and water mixture and stir until combined and a uniform, wet dough is achieved.

Grease two bread loaf pans. Sprinkle the inside with cornmeal. Spoon half the dough into each pan and then sprinkle the top with additional cornmeal. Cover the pans with oiled/sprayed plastic wrap or a damp linen towel and let rise in a warm, draft-free place until almost doubled. This will usually take about 30 to 40 minutes, depending on the conditions in your kitchen.

Bake at 400° for 20 to 25 minutes or until golden brown. Remove the loaves from the pans immediately after baking and cool completely on wire racks before cutting.

MULTIGRAIN ENGLISH MUFFIN BREAD

With just a few more ingredients (but no more work), you can make your English muffin bread a healthier, whole-grain bread. A mixture of whole wheat flour and oats added to the bread delivers a delicious, almost nutty flavor. White flour in the mix helps with the rising and softness, but if you want an even healthier whole-grain option, substitute white whole wheat flour in place of the all-purpose.

**Note: This recipe makes ONE loaf, but do feel free to double it for more to love!

- 2 C white all-purpose flour
- ⅓ C whole wheat flour
- ⅓ C wheat germ
- ⅓ C quick-cooking oats
- ½ tsp salt
- 1 TBSP sugar (or honey)
- 2 ¼ tsp (equal to 1 envelope) instant yeast
- 1 ¼ C hot water (115-120°)
- **Cornmeal (for the pan)**

In a large mixing bowl, combine the flours, oats, wheat germ, salt, sugar, and instant yeast. Stir through to combine. Pour in the hot water and stir until well-combined and a wet, soft dough forms.

Grease a bread loaf pan and sprinkle the inside with cornmeal. Spoon the dough into the pan, then sprinkle the top with additional cornmeal. Cover the pan with an oiled/sprayed piece of plastic wrap or a damp linen towel. Let rise in a warm, draft-free place until almost doubled (about 45 minutes depending on kitchen conditions).

Preheat oven to 400° during the last 10 minutes of rising. Bake for 25 to 30 minutes or until golden brown. Remove the bread from the pan immediately after baking and cool completely on a wire rack before cutting.

CLASSIC ENGLISH MUFFINS

English muffins are not something we often think about baking at home. The reality, though, is that English muffins are not more difficult than any other bread. Being able to bake them at home means being able to rid your pantry of one more preservative-laden food. These muffins freeze well, so making and baking and freezing is definitely an option. Enjoy them as a base for breakfast sandwiches or with your favorite jam or butter. One thing to know – the bubbles, nooks, and crannies of English muffins come from the dough being a wetter, stickier dough. When in doubt, err to the side of sticky with English muffin recipes.

- 1 ¼ C hot milk
- 4 to 4 ½ C all-purpose flour
- 2 tsp salt
- 1 TBSP instant yeast
- 1 egg, lightly beaten
- 2 TBSP melted butter
- Cornmeal, for working/dusting

In your microwave or on the stovetop, heat the milk to between 120° and 130°F. Set the hot milk aside and let it cool slightly to around 115°.

In a large mixing bowl, combine 4 cups of the flour, salt, and instant yeast. Stir through to combine. Add the egg, melted butter, and milk all together and then stir to mix through until the mix comes together as a uniform dough. Dough should be wet and sticky, but workable, so if needed, add the additional flour ¼ cup at a time and mix into the dough.

Turn dough out onto a well-floured surface and knead for 3 to 5 minutes. Cover kneaded dough with a clean linen cloth and let rest for 10 minutes.

After the dough has rested, sprinkle a baking sheet (with sides, preferably) generously with cornmeal. Roll or pat the dough out into a large rectangle until it is about ½ inch thick. Sprinkle more cornmeal over the top of the dough. Using a large round cutter or the rim of a large glass, cut the muffins into circles and place them on a greased or parchment-lined baking sheet (use a spatula to transfer to help hold the shape of the soft dough. Leave enough room for the muffins to rise without touching. Cover with a damp towel or oiled/sprayed plastic wrap and let rise in a warm, draft-free place until about doubled.

Towards the end of rising, preheat your oven to 350° and bake for 20-25 minutes, or until nicely browned. Cool completely before cutting.

MULTIGRAIN ENGLISH MUFFINS

Good, truly whole-grain bread and dough recipes can be hard to find, but this is one English muffin recipe that really is whole grain. It does call for soy flour, an ingredient that can be difficult to find sometimes, or that doesn't meet with everyone's dietary needs, preferences, or allergies. These muffins can easily be made without soy flour. To substitute, you can double the amount of oat flour or substitute a different whole grain flour of choice – almond flour, white whole wheat flour, chickpea flour, quinoa flour, or coconut flour are all good options.

- 2 C whole wheat flour
- 1 C oat flour
- 1 C soy flour (or substitute flour of choice)
- 2 TBSP flax seeds
- 2 TBSP instant yeast
- ½ tsp salt
- 1 TBSP oil
- 1 ¼ C hot water (115-120°)
- 1 tsp honey
- Cornmeal for dusting pan and tops

In a large mixing bowl, combine the wheat flour, oat flour, soy flour, flax seeds, instant yeast, and salt. Stir to mix through.

Add the oil, hot water, and then the honey to the dry ingredient mixture. Stir until the dough starts to come together.

Turn the dough out onto a floured surface and knead for about 6 minutes. Cover dough with a clean linen cloth and let rest for 15 minutes.

While dough is resting, prepare two baking sheets. Lightly grease each sheet and dust with cornmeal.

When dough has rested, shape the muffins. Divide the dough into 12 even balls and flatten with the palm of your hand. Place the shaped muffins on the prepared baking sheets, making sure to leave enough room for the muffins to rise without touching. Dust the tops of the muffins with cornmeal. Cover the pans with a damp towel or oiled/sprayed sheet of plastic wrap and let rise in a warm, draft-free place until doubled.

Preheat oven to 350°F and bake for 20 to 25 minutes or until done.

CINNAMON-RAISIN BREAD

It's just barely more difficult to make cinnamon raisin bread than it is to make a regular white loaf. But oh, the rewards! Warm with butter, toasted, as French toast, even a good old-fashioned bread pudding (as if there are ever enough leftovers for such a thing) ...however you serve it, this bread never disappoints.

- 2 C very warm water (115-120°F)
- ¼ C soft butter
- 6 C all-purpose flour
- 6 TBSP sugar
- 1 TBSP salt
- 2 tsp cinnamon
- 1 ½ TBSP instant yeast
- 1 ½ C raisins

Measure the warm water and add the butter to the water. Set aside.

In a large mixing bowl, combine the flour, sugar, salt, cinnamon, and instant yeast. Stir through to combine. Add in the raisins and stir once more to distribute.

Add the butter and warm water mixture and stir to combine until dough is evenly mixed and begins to come together as a ball.

Turn the dough out onto a well-floured surface and knead for 6 to 8 minutes. Dough should be smooth and elastic. Cover the kneaded dough with a clean linen cloth and let rest for 10 minutes.

Grease two bread loaf pans. Once dough has rested, cut into two even pieces and shape into two loaves. Place the loaves in the pans, seam-side down, and cover with a damp linen towel or oiled/sprayed plastic wrap. Let rise in a warm, draft-free place until doubled.

Preheat your oven to 350°F and bake for 20 to 25 minutes or until done. If desired, rub the top of the hot loaves with butter when removed from the oven for a soft, shining, buttery crust.

SWEET BANANA YEAST BREAD

Bananas in breads are more commonly known as quick-bread ingredients that are risen with leavening agents like baking powder. However, bananas are equally adept at providing moist, flavorful yeast-risen bread loaves, too. That extra moisture makes this bread easy to rise, making both new bread-makers and experienced bakers shine. (And of course – it's one more great way to use up those overripe bananas!)

- ¾ C heated milk (120°F to 130°F)
- ½ C soft butter
- 6 C all-purpose flour
- ½ C sugar
- 1 tsp salt
- 1 TBSP instant yeast
- 2 large eggs, lightly beaten
- 2 ripe mashed bananas

On your stovetop or in a microwave, heat the milk to between 120 and 130 °F. Add the butter to the hot milk and set aside. Let cool until between 115 and 120°.

In a large mixing bowl, combine the flour, sugar, salt, and instant yeast. Stir through to combine.

Add the mashed bananas and eggs. Add the water and butter mixture. Stir until well combined and dough starts to come together as a ball.

Turn the dough out onto a well-floured surface. Knead for 6 to 8 minutes until dough is smooth and elastic. If dough is too wet and sticky, knead in additional flour ¼ cup at a time. Cover the kneaded dough with a clean linen cloth and let rest for 10 minutes.

Grease two bread loaf pans. After dough has rested, divide the dough into two equal pieces and shape into two loaves. Cover with a damp linen towel or oiled/sprayed plastic wrap and let rise in a warm, draft-free place until doubled.

Preheat your oven to 375°F and bake for 40 to 45 minutes, until golden brown. If desired, rub tops of hot loaves with butter when removed from oven.

CARAMEL APPLE-PECAN BREAD

Classics flavors combine to make this sweet bread a standout. Your biggest problem will be figuring out the best time of day to enjoy it; breakfast, lunch, dinner, or tea-time, any time is a great time for a slice (even better a little warmed or toasted)!

- ½ C chopped apple (unpeeled)
- 1 C hot water (115-120°F)
- 2 TBSP softened butter
- 3 C all-purpose flour
- ¼ C packed brown sugar
- 1 tsp salt
- ¾ tsp cinnamon
- 2 tsp instant yeast
- ⅓ C toasted pecans, coarsely chopped

Core and chop the apple. Set aside.

Measure the hot water and then measure the butter into the water. Set aside.

In a large mixing bowl, combine the flour, brown sugar, salt, cinnamon, and instant yeast. Stir through to combine. Add the pecans and chopped apples and stir to distribute.

Pour the hot water and butter mixture into the flour mixture. Stir until combined and dough starts to come together as a ball.

Turn the dough out onto a well-floured surface. Knead for 6 to 8 minutes. After kneading, cover dough with a clean linen towel and let rest for 10 minutes.

Grease a bread loaf pan. When dough has rested, shape into a loaf shape and place in the prepared pan. Cover with a damp linen towel or oiled/sprayed plastic wrap. Let rise in a warm, draft-free place until doubled.

Preheat oven to 350°F and bake for 20 to 25 minutes, until nicely browned. If desired, rub the top with butter when the loaf is removed from the oven.

EASY NO-KNEAD ARTISAN-STYLE BREADS

SOME THINGS TO KNOW ABOUT SIMPLE, EASY NO-KNEAD BREADS

There truly are some incredible breads that you never have to knead at all. All you need is a little forethought of planning and the rising time. These breads turn out delicious European-style rustic loaves that are chewy and airy on the inside, laced with large nooks and crannies to cradle your butter, dipping oil, or other toppings of choice. Outside, they have that crunchy crust.

A few things to note about baking no-knead breads: Most typically use active dry yeast (ADY) rather than the instant yeast we have been working with thus far. The rising time is very long, and the long action of active dry yeast is better suited to these breads. You will note, though, that very little yeast is required for these breads; that's not a typo, for these breads it's a process of slow yeast growth similar to sourdough that works along with the natural yeasts of the flours, and that little goes a very long way. If you do not have active dry yeast in your pantry, instant yeast can be used, but the ADY will deliver the best and most reliable results (and those results are very, very reliable – it's very hard to go wrong with these breads!).

While these breads don't require kneading, they do require a very long period of rising. A little yeast over several hours gives them their rise and lift. But the time is not active time – more like a set-and-forget for a while. Plan to give this bread a minimum of 8 hours to rise. Twelve to 18 is even better (and even a bit beyond is okay if your schedule demands it). This rustic loaf uses very few ingredients; nothing could be simpler, so it's very easy to throw the dough together the night before or in the morning before you set off for the day and bake it either the next morning or the in the evening before dinner; it's a very flexible bread this way!

Finally, these breads are best when baked in a heavy cast pot like a Dutch oven with a lid. The baking method, described in the recipes that follow, is a little bit different than the norm. This use of the Dutch oven and baking at high temperatures creates the steam that bakes in that airy chewiness. Removing the lid partway through finishes the bread off with that crunchy, crusty, delicious crust. You should use a Dutch oven that is at least four quarts in size, but otherwise the size of the pot is very flexible and anything between four and eight quarts is fine to use (larger pots will result in a lower, more spread-out loaf but otherwise will still deliver a delicious bread with great taste and texture). If you do not have a Dutch oven available to you, it's well worth the investment to buy one for these breads alone – the simplicity, ease of baking, and excellent results will make this bread a new go-to. In a pinch, though, you can form this bread into a round loaf and bake it on a baking sheet with a pan of hot water on the lower rack for steam; a little less ideal, but still a good result.

Do yourself a favor and give these no-knead breads a try – I've never met a bread-eater who didn't love them!

NO-KNEAD AT ALL RUSTIC LOAF

This rustic loaf turns out an artisan-quality, round European-style bread right out of your very own oven. It is well suited as an accompaniment to any dish or dinner, and likewise with a variety of spreads and toppings (our personal household favorite – garlic and herb dipping oil!). It is a reliable sandwich bread that lasts well for days, and an easy high-quality staple to make and keep in your pantry. From bread and butter to grilled cheese, to French toast, this bread can do it all.

- **1 ½ C warm water (105 to 110°F)**
- **¼ tsp active dry yeast**
- **3 C all-purpose flour**
- **½ TBSP salt**

Measure the water into a 2-cup measuring cup. Sprinkle the yeast over the surface of the water and let sit to rehydrate for about 5 minutes.

In a large mixing bowl (one that will allow plenty of room for the dough to more than double in size), combine the flour and salt and stir through to distribute.

Stir the rehydrated yeast and water mixture and pour into the dry ingredients. Using a sturdy spoon or dough whisk, stir to combine until all ingredients are well mixed through. Dough should be on the wet and sticky side and will be looser and less formed than typical bread doughs. Make sure all flour is incorporated into the dough; you do not want a dry dough. If necessary, add more warm water, one tablespoon at a time, stirring after each addition. Add only enough water so that the dough is not dry, and the flour is completely incorporated.

After mixing, cover the bowl tightly with plastic wrap. Let sit at room temperature for 8 to 18 hours (preferably 70°F and draft-free). Dough will more than double and triple in size and will be very light and loose. There is no need to do anything with the dough during the rising time other than to make sure the wrap is tight so that no parts of it dry out.

When you are ready to bake your bread, turn the dough out onto a well-floured clean linen towel. Bring all the edges of the dough together and pinch in the middle, then gently shape around the outside of the dough to form the loaf into a round. Turn the dough over so that the seam is down. Cover the top with another clean towel and let rise for about 45 minutes to an hour.

About one-half hour into the rising process, preheat your oven and your Dutch oven: Preheat oven to 450°F. When oven is to temperature, place your empty Dutch oven, with the lid on, into your oven. Let Dutch oven preheat in the oven for 15 minutes.

When Dutch oven is preheated, carefully remove from oven. Remove the lid (some steam may escape the preheated pot, so be sure to use good oven mitts and open lid carefully). You do not need to grease your Dutch oven for this bread. Slide your hand under the towel with the loaf on it, and quickly invert it into the preheated pan. The underside, the seam-side, will now be the top of your loaf (this will split during baking and give a nice look to your bread – that is perfectly fine and is expected!). There will also be loose flour on the loaf and that is expected, too, and will give the bread a light toasted-flour coating in the end. The dough is likely to lose its shape a little when you invert it

Quick-Time Homemade Bread and Pastries

into the pan. This is also expected. Give the pan a gentle shake to help re-form and center the dough, but do not do anything further – the dough will rise and reshape itself as it bakes. Place the lid back on the Dutch oven (use a mitt!!) and place the Dutch oven back in the oven.

Bake the loaf for 30 minutes. After 30 minutes, remove the lid only (be careful, obviously use mitts, and open the pot away from you – steam will escape when you remove the lid). Bake with the lid off for an additional 15 minutes to finish browning the crust.

When bread is done baking, carefully remove from the oven and gently turn out onto a wire rack. Using oven mitts, turn the bread over on the rack, right-side-up, and let cool.

GARLIC & HERB DIPPING OIL

This dipping oil is the perfect sidecar for artisan-style no-knead breads. It is an ideal companion for other loaves like French bread, Italian, baguettes, and more. It takes only moments to mix but is always a crowd-pleaser...or...perfect for dinner for just one or two. (Incidentally, a simple basket with a loaf of fresh homemade bread and a jar of dipping oil is always a HUGE hit as a gift or dinner contribution!)

- 1 C olive oil
- 2 tsp dried minced garlic (or 2 cloves fresh garlic, finely chopped)
- ½ tsp dry parsley (or 1 tsp fresh, chopped)
- ½ tsp dry thyme (or 1 tsp fresh, chopped)
- ½ tsp dry basil (or 1 tsp fresh, chopped)
- ½ tsp dry marjoram (or 1 tsp fresh, chopped)
- ¼ tsp sea salt (optional)
- ¼ tsp cracked black pepper (optional)
- *Can substitute other favorite herbs, such as chives, dill, bay, oregano, rosemary, cilantro, dried chili peppers, red pepper flakes...
- *Can add ¼ to ½ cup good balsamic vinegar if desired

Combine all ingredients together in a clean jar. Cap, gently shake, and let sit to infuse for several hours.

If using fresh garlic or herbs to infuse your oil, fresh herbs need to be strained out. Strain oil through a fine-mesh strainer after three hours. Dry herbs and garlic may be left in the oil.

Let the oil sit out at room temperature for three hours to infuse flavors, then serve or refrigerate. Refrigerate any extra oil. Infused oil can be kept for up to one week in the refrigerator (oil is less likely to harden if stored on the door – if hardening occurs, simply set out at room temperature a half hour before use). Oil may be made ahead if properly stored in the refrigerator and used within one week.

Oil also makes an excellent base for salad dressing, tossed with pasta, or mixed with an equal amount of good vinegar of choice and used as a meat marinade.

SEASONED HERB BUTTER

Seasoned butters or herb butters are technically called "compound butters," though there is nothing compound or complex about making them at all. You should feel free to use virtually any favorite herb or combination of herbs. Serving these butters alongside your fresh, homemade breads will make both you and your efforts shine!

- ½ C butter, well-softened (salted or unsalted as preferred)
- ⅛ C dried herb or a mix of dried herbs of choice (or ¼ C fresh)
- 3 tsp dry minced garlic (or 5 cloves fresh garlic; optional)
- 1 tsp lemon juice (optional)

To prepare, place very soft butter in a small mixing bowl. Add garlic and herbs. Work through with a spatula until thoroughly combined.

Spoon herbed butter into a small ramekin or serving bowl. Cover and place in refrigerator to harden. Alternatively, you can spoon the butter out onto a sheet of waxed paper and roll the butter into a log. Wrap the roll in the waxed paper (or a fresh sheet if preferred), place the covered roll in a Tupperware container or zipper bag, and refrigerate until ready to use. Refrigerate at least several hours before first use to allow flavors to combine. If desired, cut rolled butter into individual pats before serving.

Compound herb butters can be made in an almost unlimited variety of flavors. Some favorite combinations include:

- garlic and basil
- chive butter
- garlic and parsley
- basil, parsley, and thyme
- tarragon and parsley
- mint butter (ideal for serving with lamb)
- sage and marjoram (ideal for poultry)

In addition to serving as a spread for breads, compound butters are also delicious when brushed on grilled or roasted meats, or with a pat served on top of steaks, roasts, and cuts. Likewise, they make delicious spreads for making garlic bread, toast, for seasoning vegetables, or as an upscale seasoning in mashed potatoes.

NO-KNEAD RUSTIC SOURDOUGH LOAF

To be clear, you will need a started, fed sourdough starter to make this bread. Sourdough starters are easy to make (as in, flour and water) and to maintain. You will find plenty of recipes and instructions online, and you can even buy portions of fresh starter that you can feed up, keep, maintain, and use for all your bread and baking needs (because yes, sourdough is for more than just bread!). Sourdough is a traditional, natural way to leaven (rise) bread that delivers more health and digestion benefits than many yeast-risen breads. It can be rather fun and addicting, too (some people have even been known to name their starters!). Don't be intimidated – give sourdough a try!

- 3 ½ C all-purpose white flour
- 2 tsp salt
- ¼ C fed sourdough starter
- 1 ½ C lukewarm water

In a large mixing bowl (large enough for the dough to double and possibly triple in size), combine the flour and salt and stir through to evenly distribute ingredients. Add the sourdough starter and the water. Mix until evenly combined, making sure all flour is evenly incorporated (if necessary, add additional water one tablespoon at a time and stir after each addition – only enough to bring all the flour into the mix).

Cover the dough tightly with plastic wrap and let rise in a warm, draft-free place for at least 8 hours, and up to as much as 18 to 24.

When ready to bake, turn the dough out onto a well-floured clean linen towel. Bring all the edges of the dough together and pinch in the middle, then gently shape around the outside of the dough to form the loaf into a round. Turn the dough over so that the seam is underneath. Cover the top with another clean towel and let rise for about 45 minutes to an hour.

One-half hour into the rising process, preheat your oven and your Dutch oven: Preheat oven to 450°F. When oven is to temperature, place your empty Dutch oven, with the lid on, into your oven. Let Dutch oven preheat in the oven for 15 minutes.

When Dutch oven is preheated, carefully remove from oven. Remove the lid (some steam may escape the preheated pot, so be sure to use good oven mitts and open lid carefully). You do not need to grease your Dutch oven for this bread. Slide your hand under the towel with the loaf on it, and quickly invert the loaf into the preheated pan. The underside (the seam-side) will now be the top of your loaf (this will split during baking and give a nice look to your bread – is expected!). There will also be loose flour on the loaf and that is expected, too, and will give the bread a light toasted-flour coating in the end. The dough is likely to lose its shape a little when you invert it into the pan. This is also expected. Give the pan a gentle shake to help re-form and center the dough, but do not do anything further – the dough will rise and reshape itself as it bakes. Place the lid back on the Dutch oven (use a mitt!!) and place the Dutch oven back in the oven.

Bake the loaf for 30 minutes. After 30 minutes, remove the lid only (be careful, obviously use mitts, and open the pot away from you – steam will escape when you remove the lid). Bake with the lid off for an additional 15 minutes to finish browning the crust.

When bread is done baking, carefully remove from the oven and gently turn out onto a wire rack. Using oven mitts or a clean towel (bread will be hot!), turn the bread over on the rack, right-side-up, and let cool.

*To make a wheat version of this sourdough bread, use half all-purpose flour and half whole wheat flour. You may also use white whole wheat flour and/or a mixture of half white whole wheat and half whole wheat flour for a whole grain wheat sourdough. The recommended rising time for more dense wheat breads is 12-18 hours.

NO-KNEAD WHEAT & OAT WHOLEGRAIN SOURDOUGH LOAF

Looking for a little whole grain in an easy, no-knead sourdough? This is your bread! Again, you'll need a fed sourdough starter to make this recipe, which gives you all the goodness and texture of a sourdough artisan loaf without the work. This loaf makes two slightly smaller loaves, but if you have a large Dutch oven (8 to 10+ quarts) feel free to bake it as one large loaf.

- 4 C whole wheat white flour (can substitute all-purpose)
- 2 C whole wheat flour
- 1 C oat flour
- ½ C whole oats
- 4 tsp salt
- (optional) pinch of instant yeast
- ½ C fed sourdough starter
- 3 ¼ C lukewarm water

In a large mixing bowl, combine the white flour, whole wheat flour, oat flour, whole oats, and salt (if using a pinch of instant yeast for an extra boost in rising, add it now). Stir through to evenly distribute. Add the sourdough starter and water all together and then stir until combined.

Be sure that all flour is incorporated. If dough is too dry and flour remnants will not mix in, add water one tablespoon at a time, just until a consistent dough is achieved (but do not make it too wet). Cover the bowl tightly with plastic wrap and let rise in a warm, draft-free place for a minimum of 8 hours, up to 24.

When you are ready to bake your bread, turn the dough out onto a well-floured clean linen towel. Bring all the edges of the dough together and pinch in the middle, then gently shape around the outside of the dough to form the loaf into a round. Turn the dough over so that the seam is down. Cover the top with another clean towel and let rise for about 45 minutes to an hour.

One-half hour into the rising process, preheat your oven and your Dutch oven: Preheat oven to 450°F. When oven is to temperature, place your empty Dutch oven, with the lid on, into your oven. Let Dutch oven preheat in the oven for 15 minutes.

When Dutch oven is preheated, carefully remove from oven. Remove the lid (some steam may escape the preheated pot, so be sure to use good oven mitts and open lid carefully). You do not need to grease your Dutch oven for this bread. Slide your hand under the towel with the loaf on it, and quickly invert it into the preheated pan. The underside (the seam-side) will now be the top of your loaf (this will split during baking and give a nice look to your bread – that is expected!). There will also be loose flour on the loaf. That is expected, too, and will give the bread a light toasted-flour coating in the end. The dough is likely to lose its shape a little when you invert it into the pan. This is also expected. Give the pan a gentle shake to help re-form and center the dough, but do not do anything further – the dough will rise and reshape itself as it bakes. Place the lid back on the Dutch oven (use a mitt!!) and place the Dutch oven back in the oven.

Bake the loaf for 30 minutes. After 30 minutes, remove the lid only (be careful, obviously use mitts, and open the pot away from you – steam will escape when you remove the lid). Bake with the lid off for an additional 15 minutes to finish browning the crust.

When bread is done baking, carefully remove from the oven and gently turn out onto a wire rack. Using oven mitts or a clean towel (bread will be hot!), turn the bread over on the rack, right-side-up, and let cool.

NO-KNEAD HONEY-OAT WHEAT BREAD

This recipe is very similar to the preceding recipe, except that you do not need a sourdough starter, and the addition of honey delivers some sweetness that works nicely with the whole grains. Incidentally, for a slightly darker loaf with a little different flavor, feel free to substitute molasses for the honey in this recipe. Bake as one large or two smaller loaves

- 3 ¼ C warm water
- ½ C honey
- ½ tsp active dry yeast
- 4 C white whole wheat flour (can substitute all-purpose)
- 2 C whole wheat flour
- 1 C oat flour
- ½ C whole oats
- 4 tsp salt

Measure out the warm water and honey and sprinkle the yeast over the top to rehydrate. Set aside.

In a large mixing bowl, combine the white whole wheat, whole wheat, oat flour, whole oats, and salt. Stir through to evenly distribute. Add the warm water and honey mixture all together. Mix well until all ingredients and all flours are incorporated. If there is still dry flour in the bowl, add additional water 1 tablespoon at a time, just until you have a moist, uniform dough, not too wet but not at all dry. Cover the bowl tightly and leave it to rise in a warm, draft-free place for a minimum of 8 hours, and up to 24.

When you are ready to bake your bread, turn the dough out onto a well-floured clean linen towel. Bring all the edges of the dough together and pinch in the middle, then gently shape around the outside of the dough to form the loaf into a round. Turn the dough over so that the seam is underneath. Cover the top with another clean towel and let rise for about 45 minutes to an hour.

One-half hour into the rising process, preheat your oven and your Dutch oven: Preheat oven to 450°F. When oven is to temperature, place your empty Dutch oven, with the lid on, into your oven. Let Dutch oven preheat in the oven for 15 minutes.

When Dutch oven is preheated, carefully remove from oven. Remove the lid (some steam may escape the preheated pot, so be sure to use good oven mitts and open lid carefully). You do not need to grease your Dutch oven for this bread. Slide your hand under the towel with the loaf on it, and quickly invert it into the preheated pan. The underside (the seam-side) will now be the top of your loaf (this will split during baking and give a nice look to your bread – that is perfectly fine and is expected!). There will also be loose flour on the loaf and that is expected, too. It will give the bread a light toasted-flour coating in the end. The dough is likely to lose its shape a little when you invert it into the pan. This is fine, too, and expected. Give the pan a gentle shake to help re-form and center the dough, but do not do anything further – the dough will rise and reshape itself as it bakes. Place the lid back on the Dutch oven (use a mitt!!) and place the Dutch oven back in the oven.

Bake the loaf for 30 minutes. After 30 minutes, remove the lid only (be careful, obviously use mitts, and open the pot away from you--steam

will escape when you remove the lid). Bake with the lid off for an additional 15 minutes to finish browning the crust.

When bread is done baking, carefully remove from the oven and gently turn out onto a wire rack. Using oven mitts or a clean towel (bread will be hot!), turn the bread over on the rack, right-side-up, and let cool.

NO-KNEAD MULTIGRAIN ARTISAN LOAF

Another excellent option for whole grains in an easy loaf, this loaf brings you a little of that rye flavor that is so well-loved. White all-purpose flour helps in the rising, but as always, for a truly whole-grain bread, feel free to substitute white whole wheat flour for the all-purpose. This recipe will make one large loaf in an eight quart or larger Dutch oven or can be split into two smaller rounds.

- 3 ¼ C lukewarm water
- ½ tsp active dry yeast
- 3 C all-purpose white flour (or substitute white whole wheat)
- 1 ½ C whole wheat flour
- 1 ½ C rye flour
- ½ C rolled oats (can substitute sunflower seeds, nuts, wheat germ, or cracked wheat, etc.)
- 1 TBSP salt

Measure the warm water and sprinkle the yeast over the top to rehydrate and proof. Set aside.

In a large mixing bowl (large enough for the dough to more than double), combine the white flour, wheat flour, rye flour, oats, and salt.

Stir through to combine and evenly distribute. Pour in the water and yeast mixture. Mix until thoroughly combined, making sure that all the flour is incorporated. If necessary, add water 1 tablespoon at a time until all flour is mixed, and dough is uniform. Dough should be slightly wet and sticky, but not too wet (no standing water in the bowl). Cover the bowl tightly and let rise in a warm, draft-free place for at least 8 hours, up to 24.

When you are ready to bake your bread, turn the dough out onto a well-floured, clean linen towel. Bring all the edges of the dough together and pinch in the middle, then gently shape around the outside of the dough to form the loaf into a round. Turn the dough over so that the seam is underneath. Cover the top with another clean towel and let rise for about 45 minutes to an hour.

One-half hour into the rising process, preheat your oven and your Dutch oven: Preheat oven to 450°F. When oven is to temperature, place your empty Dutch oven, with the lid on, into your oven. Let Dutch oven preheat in the oven for 15 minutes.

When Dutch oven is preheated, carefully remove from oven. Remove the lid (some steam may escape the preheated pot, so be sure to use good oven mitts and open lid carefully). You do not need to grease your Dutch oven for this bread. Slide your hand under the towel with the loaf on it, and quickly invert it into the preheated pan. The underside (the seam-side) will now be the top of your loaf (this will split during baking and give a nice look to your bread – that is perfectly fine and is expected!). There will also be loose flour on the loaf and that is expected, too. It will give the bread a light toasted-flour coating in the end. The dough is likely to lose its shape a little when you invert it into the pan. This is also expected. Give the pan a gentle shake to help re-form and center the dough, but do not do anything further – the dough will rise and reshape itself as it bakes. Place the lid back on the Dutch oven (use a mitt!!) and place the Dutch oven back in the oven.

Bake the loaf for 30 minutes. After 30 minutes, remove the lid only (be careful, obviously use mitts, and open the pot away from you – steam

will escape when you remove the lid). Bake with the lid off for an additional 15 minutes to finish browning the crust.

When bread is done baking, carefully remove from the oven and gently turn out onto a wire rack. Using oven mitts or a clean towel (bread will be hot!), turn the bread over on the rack, right-side-up, and let cool.

NO-KNEAD CHUNKY CHOCOLATE CHERRY ALMOND BREAD

This easy no-knead recipe is huge on flavor. A bit of chocolate, a touch of sweet-tart cherries, and balanced with the tang of rye, it's bread enough to be served with dinner, but treat enough to taste with tea. It makes a fabulous toast and shines with warming. Need a gift? Holiday dinner contribution? This bread can't fail. There is no time that isn't good for this bread, and it's just as easy to make as any other no-knead.

- 1 ½ C lukewarm water
- ½ tsp active dry yeast
- 3 C all-purpose white flour
- ½ C whole wheat flour
- ½ C rye flour
- 1 TBSP orange peel (optional)
- 2 ½ tsp salt
- 1 ¼ C sliced almonds, toasted (or substitute preferred nut: pecans, walnuts, or mix recommended)
- ¾ C sweetened dried cherries
- ½ C semi-sweet or dark chocolate chunks or chips

Toast nuts on a baking sheet for 10-12 minutes at 350°F. Set aside.

Measure warm water and sprinkle yeast over the top to rehydrate and proof. Set aside.

In a large mixing bowl (large enough for dough to more than double), combine white flour, wheat flour, rye flour, orange peel, and salt. Stir through to evenly distribute. Now add the toasted nuts, cherries, and chocolate chunks. Stir through to combine.

Pour in the water and yeast mixture, and then stir until dough is evenly mixed and no flour remains in the bowl. Dough should be on the wet and sticky side. If dough appears dry or if there is still flour in the bottom of the bowl, add water 1 tablespoon at a time, mixing after each addition, until dough is uniform, and all ingredients are incorporated. Cover bowl tightly with plastic wrap and let rise in a warm, draft-free place for a minimum of 8 hours, up to 24.

When you are ready to bake your bread, turn the dough out onto a well-floured clean linen towel. Bring all the edges of the dough together and pinch in the middle, then gently shape around the outside of the dough to form the loaf into a round. Turn the dough over so that the seam is underneath. Cover the top with another clean towel and let rise for about 45 minutes to an hour.

One-half hour into the rising process, preheat your oven and your Dutch oven: Preheat oven to 450°F. When oven is to temperature, place your empty Dutch oven, with the lid on, into your oven. Let Dutch oven preheat in the oven for 15 minutes.

When Dutch oven is preheated, carefully remove from oven. Remove the lid (some steam may escape the preheated pot, so be sure to use good oven mitts and open lid carefully). You do not need to grease your Dutch oven for this bread. Slide your hand under the towel with the loaf on it, and quickly invert it into the preheated pan. The underside (the seam-side) will now be the top of your loaf (this will split during baking and give a nice look to your bread – that is perfectly fine and is expected!). There will also be loose flour on the loaf and that is expected, too. It will give the bread a light toasted-flour coating in the end. The dough is likely to lose its shape a little when you invert it into the pan. This is fine also expected. Give the pan a gentle shake to help re-form and center the dough, but do not do anything further – the dough will rise and reshape itself as it bakes. Place the lid back on the Dutch oven (use a mitt!!) and place the Dutch oven back in the oven.

Bake the loaf for 30 minutes. After 30 minutes, remove the lid only (be careful, obviously use mitts, and open the pot away from you – steam will escape when you remove the lid). Bake with the lid off for an additional 15 minutes to finish browning the crust.

When bread is done baking, carefully remove from the oven and gently turn out onto a wire rack. Using oven mitts or a clean towel (bread will be hot!), turn the bread over on the rack, right-side-up, and let cool.

NO-KNEAD CHEESE BREAD

For a bread with a lot of flavor, this recipe couldn't be easier. Your basic, delicious no-knead recipe, but with cheese! As far as the cheese goes, there are a few recommendations here, but do feel free to play. It's hard to imagine a cheese that WOULDN'T be good nestled in that home of warm, chewy goodness!

- **3 C lukewarm water**
- **½ tsp active dry yeast**
- **6 C all-purpose flour**
- **1 TBSP salt**
- **2 C shredded or grated cheese of choice (cheddar, parmesan, or Asiago recommended)**

Measure the water and sprinkle the yeast over the top to rehydrate. Set aside.

In a large mixing bowl (large enough for the dough to more than double), combine the flour, salt, and grated cheese. Stir through so that all is evenly distributed.

Pour in the water and yeast mixture. Mix the dough well until all ingredients are combined and a sticky, loose dough is achieved. Make sure that all the flour is incorporated into the dough. If it is not, add additional water 1 tablespoon at a time, stirring after each addition. Only add as much water as it takes for all the flour to mix in and make a uniform dough. Cover tightly and let rise in a warm, draft-free place for a minimum of 6 to 8 hours but as long as 18 hours, until ready to bake.

When you are ready to bake your bread, turn the dough out onto a well-floured clean linen towel. Bring all the edges of the dough together and pinch in the middle, then gently shape around the outside of the dough to form the loaf into a round. Turn the dough over so that the seam is underneath. Cover the top with another clean towel and let rise for about 45 minutes to an hour.

One-half hour into the rising process, preheat your oven and your Dutch oven: Preheat oven to 450°F. When oven is to temperature, place your empty Dutch oven, with the lid on, into your oven. Let Dutch oven preheat in the oven for 15 minutes.

When Dutch oven is preheated, carefully remove from oven. Remove the lid (some steam may escape the preheated pot, so be sure to use good oven mitts and open lid carefully). You do not need to grease your Dutch oven for this bread. Slide your hand under the towel with the loaf on it, and quickly invert it into the preheated pan. The underside (the seam-side) will now be the top of your loaf (this will split during baking and give a nice look to your bread – that is perfectly fine and is expected!). There will also be loose flour on the loaf and that is expected, too. It will give the bread a light toasted-flour coating in the end. The dough is likely to lose its shape a little when you invert it into the pan. This is also expected. Give the pan a gentle shake to help re-form and center the dough, but do not do anything further – the dough will rise and reshape itself as it bakes. Place the lid back on the Dutch oven (use a mitt!!) and place the Dutch oven back in the oven.

Bake the loaf for 30 minutes. After 30 minutes, remove the lid only (be careful, obviously use mitts, and open the pot away from you – steam

will escape when you remove the lid). Bake with the lid off for an additional 15 minutes to finish browning the crust.

When bread is done baking, carefully remove from the oven and gently turn out onto a wire rack. Using oven mitts or a clean towel (bread will be hot!), turn the bread over on the rack, right-side-up, and let cool.

NO-KNEAD ARTISAN HERB LOAF

So savory, so simple, so many great options in subtly-flavored bread to share and enjoy, and to make you shine (it's okay to go ahead and brag a little!). This herb bread is quite versatile, and all it takes to make it is adding in some herbs to your basic no-knead bread recipe. Use the herbs suggested here, but also experiment if you like with your favorite herb combinations. Add in the garlic for the simplest garlic-herb bread ever. Another great option? Add in the cheese from the previous recipe, for a no-knead cheese and herb bread!

- 3 C lukewarm water
- ½ tsp active dry yeast
- 6 C all-purpose flour
- 1 TBSP salt
- 2 TBSP dried minced garlic or garlic flakes (optional; double measure for fresh)
- 1 scant TBSP dried rosemary
- 1 scant TBSP dried oregano
- 1 scant TBSP dried basil
- 1 scant TBSP dried thyme

Measure the water and sprinkle the yeast over the top to rehydrate. Set aside.

In a large mixing bowl (large enough for the dough to more than double), combine the flour, salt, garlic, and herbs. Stir through so that all is evenly distributed.

Pour in the water and yeast mixture. Mix the dough well until all ingredients are combined and a sticky, loose dough is achieved. Make sure that all the flour is incorporated into the dough. If it is not, add additional water 1 tablespoon at a time, stirring after each addition. Only add as much water as it takes for all the flour to mix in and make a uniform dough. Cover tightly and let rise in a warm, draft-free place for a minimum of 6 to 8 hours but as long as 18 hours, until ready to bake.

When you are ready to bake your bread, turn the dough out onto a well-floured clean linen towel. Bring all the edges of the dough together and pinch in the middle, then gently shape around the outside of the dough to form the loaf into a round. Turn the dough over so that the seam is underneath. Cover the top with another clean towel and let rise for about 45 minutes to an hour.

One-half hour into the rising process, preheat your oven and your Dutch oven: Preheat oven to 450°F. When oven is to temperature, place your empty Dutch oven, with the lid on, into your oven. Let Dutch oven preheat in the oven for 15 minutes.

When Dutch oven is preheated, carefully remove from oven. Remove the lid (some steam may escape the preheated pot, so be sure to use good oven mitts and open lid carefully). You do not need to grease your Dutch oven for this bread. Slide your hand under the towel with the loaf on it, and quickly invert it into the preheated pan. The underside (the seam-side) will now be the top of your loaf (this will split during baking and give a nice look to your bread – that is perfectly fine and is expected!). There will also be loose flour on the loaf and that is expected, too. This will give the bread a light toasted-flour coating in the end. The dough is likely to lose its shape a little when you invert it into the pan. This is also expected. Give the pan a gentle shake to help re-form and center the dough, but do not do anything further – the dough will rise and reshape itself as it bakes. Place the lid back on the Dutch oven (use a mitt!!) and place the Dutch oven back in the oven.

Bake the loaf for 30 minutes. After 30 minutes, remove the lid only (be careful, obviously use mitts, and open the pot away from you – steam will escape when you remove the lid). Bake with the lid off for an additional 15 minutes to finish browning the crust.

When bread is done baking, carefully remove from the oven and gently turn out onto a wire rack. Using oven mitts or a clean towel (bread will be hot!), turn the bread over on the rack, right-side-up, and let cool.

ODDS & ENDS FAVORITES

PITA POCKETS

It's always nice to have something a little different in your portfolio. These pita pockets have the advantage of being light and versatile for anything from pocket sandwiches to an accompaniment for salads, dips, and hummus. (Tip: Cut leftover pockets into wedges or slices and toast in the oven until crisp for a wholesome, preservative-free chip and cracker option.)

- 2 C all-purpose white flour
- 1 ⅓ C whole wheat flour
- 4 tsp sugar (or honey)
- 1 ½ tsp salt
- 1 ½ tsp instant yeast
- 1 ⅓ C very warm water
- 3 TBSP olive oil

In a large mixing bowl, combine the white flour, wheat flour, sugar, salt, and instant yeast. Stir through to combine.

Pour in the warm water and olive oil all together. Stir until dough is combined and comes together as a uniform ball. Cover the bowl with a clean linen cloth and let rest for 10 minutes.

Prepare 2 baking sheets. Lightly oil or spray the sheets with baking spray.

After the dough has rested, turn the dough out onto a floured surface. Divide the dough into 10 even pieces and shape into balls. Space 5 balls out onto each prepared baking sheet. Cover with a damp linen towel or oiled/sprayed plastic wrap and let rise in a warm, draft-free place for 20 minutes.

About ten minutes into the rising period, preheat your oven to 500°F.

After rising, shape the balls into rounds to make the pocket breads: Using your fingertips, flatten each ball out into a 6-inch circle.

Bake for 5 minutes, until tops puff and begin to brown. Cool completely before cutting. For pocket breads, cut pitas in half.

SOFT PRETZELS

Quite possibly the perfect recipe to have on hand for snacking or party planning, these soft pretzels are always a hit. One of those snacks you can never seem to make enough of. Gameday, movie night, party buffet, served with mustards and dips, or just enjoyed solo...these pretzels are never wrong. (Note: See the variations at the end for even more easy and versatile pretzel preparations.)

- 1 egg yolk
- 3 ½ C all-purpose white flour
- 2 TBSP sugar
- 2 tsp instant yeast
- 1 tsp salt
- ⅛ tsp white pepper (or finely-ground black pepper)
- 1 ¼ C very warm water
- 1 TBSP olive oil

For the glaze:

- 1 egg white
- 1 TBSP water

Optional topping suggestions:

- coarse salt
- sesame seeds
- grated cheese
- garlic powder or minced dried garlic
- dry minced onion
- bacon bits
- drizzled melted chocolate or caramel
- combinations of above

Separate one egg. Lightly beat the yolk and set aside. Reserve the white for the glaze.

In a large mixing bowl, combine the flour, sugar, instant yeast, salt, and pepper. Stir through to evenly distribute. Add the water, egg yolk, and oil all at once. Stir until evenly mixed and dough comes together as a uniform ball.

Turn the dough out onto a lightly floured surface and knead for 6 to 8 minutes. Cover with a clean linen towel and let rest for 10 minutes.

While the dough rests, prepare the baking sheet: Lightly grease or oil the sheet. Prepare the glaze and set aside: Whisk water and egg white together. Gather toppings of choice, if using.

After dough has rested, shape the pretzels. Cut dough into about 16 even pieces. Roll each piece into a rope 15-16 inches long. Make a loop in the middle of the rope. Cross the ends of the rope and twist once. Fold the twisted end back over the loop to form a pretzel shape. Lightly press twist into the loop to hold in place. Place formed pretzels on the prepared baking sheet, spacing about 1 ½ inches apart.

After all pretzels are shaped, brush with the glaze and sprinkle toppings over the glaze. Cover lightly with a damp linen towel or oiled/sprayed plastic wrap and let rise in a warm, draft-free place until doubled (about ½ hour).

Preheat your oven to 375°F. Bake for 15 to 20 minutes or until done and nicely browned.

*Easy Pretzel Bites: To make even easier, bite-sized pretzels for a crowd or for simple snacking, prepare as above, but instead of twisting the pretzels into pretzel shapes, cut ropes into evenly-sized pieces, about ½ to 1 inch long. Rise and prepare as per instructions.

**Pepperoni Pretzels: For a flavored pepperoni pretzel, add 1 cup of thin-sliced pepperoni, cut into quarters, and ⅛ cup grated parmesan cheese to the dry ingredients. Prepare as instructed.

READY-FAST PIZZA DOUGH

Every kitchen should have a good, reliable standby pizza dough recipe. Naturally, it's the perfect dough for making homemade pizza, but this recipe makes a great base for making sweet or savory breadsticks, too. Any way you top it, you'll be glad to have this quick and easy pizza dough recipe around.

- 5 C white all-purpose flour
- 1 TBSP salt
- 1 TBSP instant yeast
- 2 C very warm water
- olive oil for pan
- cornmeal for pan (optional)

In a large mixing bowl, combine the flour, salt, and instant yeast. Stir through to evenly distribute.

Pour in the water and mix until combined and dough comes together as a ball.

Turn the dough out onto a floured surface and knead for about 6 minutes until dough is smooth and uniform. Work in a few extra tablespoons of flour if needed. Cover with a clean linen towel and let rest for 10 minutes.

Meanwhile, place your oven racks in the middle and top of your oven and preheat your oven to 350°F. Prepare two pizza pans or sheet pans. To prep the pans, lightly coat them with olive oil and then sprinkle the oiled surface with cornmeal.

When the dough has rested, divide it into 2 even pieces. Place each piece on a prepared pan and stretch it to fill the pan, taking care not to rip holes in the dough. (If you do rip the dough, simply pinch the holes back together.) If the dough is snapping back too much, give the piece a rest while you work on the other pan and come back to it; it should lose some of that elasticity and stretch more easily.

It is best to par-bake the pizza dough so that your pizza does not come out too soft and doughy. Place the prepared doughs in the oven at 350°F and bake for 7 minutes. Remove from oven and increase oven temperature to 400°F.

Top par-baked pizza doughs as desired. Return to oven and bake for 10 minutes more, or until done.

WHOLE WHEAT PIZZA DOUGH

Yes, we are all getting just a little more health-conscious these days. The beautiful thing is that with good, wholesome, preservative-free bread and dough recipes that include more whole grains, we don't have to give up all that we know and love. This whole-wheat pizza dough recipe is a perfect example. As with many whole-wheat and whole grain recipes, it includes a mix of white flour and whole wheat flour, but you can always exchange the white all-purpose for white whole wheat to increase the whole grains and fiber in the recipe.

- 1 ½ C white all-purpose flour (or white whole wheat)
- 1 C whole wheat flour
- 1 TBSP sugar
- 1 tsp salt
- 2 tsp instant yeast
- 1 C very warm water
- 2 TBSP olive oil
- cornmeal for pan (optional)

In a large mixing bowl, combine the white flour, wheat flour, sugar, salt, and instant yeast. Stir through to evenly distribute.

Pour the water and olive oil in together and mix until combined, and the dough comes together as a ball.

Turn the dough out onto a floured surface and knead for about 6 minutes until dough is smooth and uniform. Work in a few extra tablespoons of flour if needed. Cover with a clean linen towel and let rest for 10 minutes.

Meanwhile, place your oven rack in the middle of your oven and preheat your oven to 350°F. Prepare one pizza pan or sheet pan. To prep the pan, lightly coat with olive oil and then sprinkle the oiled surface with cornmeal.

When the dough has rested, divide it into 2 even pieces. Place each piece on a prepared pan and stretch it to fill the pan, taking care not to rip holes in the dough. (If you do rip the dough, simply pinch the holes back together.) If the dough is snapping back too much, give the piece a rest for a few minutes and come back to it; it should lose some of that elasticity and stretch more easily.

It is best to par-bake the pizza dough so that your pizza does not come out too soft and doughy. Place the prepared dough in the oven at 350°F and bake for 7 minutes. Remove from oven and increase oven temperature to 400°F.

Top par-baked pizza dough as desired. Return to oven and bake for 10 minutes more, or until done.

TROUBLESHOOTING QUICK-TIME BASIC BREADS

Earlier we talked about the fact that the bread-baking experience is, to an extent, going to be different for every baker, and in fact, will be different in different regions and even in different kitchens. Still, sometimes things just don't go as planned and a few troubleshooting tips and tricks can help you sort out what might have gone wrong so that the next time around can be a raging success!

Most difficulties in bread baking are with the rise, and most issues with rising are easily solved. When your dough doesn't want to rise, look to these factors for fixes:

- **Check your yeast.** Most rise issues come down to the yeast. Is it old or expired? Where do you store it? Is your storage area too warm? Too moist? In these cases, the yeast may have already acted out its yeasty life and not have a lot left to give to your bread.

  If your pantry or cabinets are too warm or humid, store yeast in a zipper bag or sealed storage container in the freezer until ready to use (especially an issue in summer months). Replace any yeast that has been hanging around a while. You may want to switch yeast brands altogether. It's just a fact that some brands are better than others and your issue could be as simple as the brand of yeast you're buying. Also, consider the seller – maybe *they* are keeping *their* stock around too long, or improperly storing it before sale. If it seems like the brand isn't the issue, try buying your yeast from someone else.

- **Use more yeast.** Don't increase it by a lot, but maybe your particular yeast brand just needs a little more to get things going. Try increasing the yeast in the recipe by a good pinch or ¼ teaspoon and see if that helps. Just don't try to increase the yeast too much to solve a rising issue – you shouldn't see that much variation between yeast brands, and excessive yeast amounts will make things rise too fast, lose structure, and fall. Too much yeast will also result in a very yeasty flavor that you probably won't enjoy.

- **Try a longer kneading time.** Kneading is an important part of the mixing and gluten-development process. If you fail to knead your dough for a long enough period of time to thoroughly mix the ingredients and to start the development of the gluten, the result is often inferior rising and/or inferior bread structure and texture. Six to eight minutes is the usual recommended time for kneading so if you need to, set a timer for at least six minutes to make sure you get enough kneading time in. If you know you're kneading a solid six minutes, go to eight and maybe even ten. Theoretically, over-kneading can cause the same problems, but it's nearly impossible for a human being to over-knead dough that much without first becoming exhausted. It's said that even a stand mixer would have a hard time accomplishing that.

- **How humid is your kitchen?** Bread needs humidity in order to rise, so if you're working in a very dry climate or dry kitchen, you may need to do something to increase the environmental humidity. This is a particular problem in the winter months. You can do this in a few ways: Simmer a pot or kettle of water on a stovetop to increase the room's humidity level; run a household humidifier before and during bread making; let the bread rise inside a controlled environment, like your oven, and introduce humidity.

To do this, turn your oven on to "warm" or set at a low temperature (175-190°F) while you mix and prepare the dough. Heat a kettle of water to boiling as you work. After you have rested, shaped, and placed the dough in pans, turn the oven off and put the pans of dough on the uppermost rack of the oven, placed in the middle (do not cover the dough with a towel or plastic wrap during rising when you use this method). Place a baking pan or large oven-proof skillet on the bottom rack of your oven and fill it with the hot water. Close the oven and leave closed until risen to double. Only open the door to check the level of the rise. Bread can rise very quickly this way (in fact it's a good way to rush rising and speed up the bread-baking process when time is short). Check the rising dough after about 20 minutes.

- **Find the best place to rise.** Bread needs warm, draft-free places to rise that are not too dry. Your kitchen may or may not be the best location in your home. Or, a certain spot in your kitchen may be better than another. Seek out the places that provide the best environment. Just be aware that if the spot is *too* hot, baking might occur before rising – so too near the vent of a preheating oven or too close to a fireplace or woodstove might not be better.

- **Over-rising is not better.** When you let bread rise too far, the structure becomes unstable and falls at the slightest bump or transfer to the oven. Be aware of this and don't let your rise go too far. The rule of thumb is double the dough size and springing back at a light press of the top of the loaf. In most bread pans this is about an inch over the rim of the pan, but do realize that, that is an inch to the top of the *rounded arch* of the loaf over the pan's edge. It might look a little on the low side, but you should also get some "oven spring" when the bread is baked that will result in a little more rising and height.

- **Lighten up your measuring.** Bread texture and density issues, and sometimes rising issues, are sometimes because we are inadvertently using too much of an ingredient, usually flour. I do cheat and measure right out of the canister with a one-cup measure most of the time and it works out most of the time, but sometimes a particular flour brand is dense or settles a lot in shipping, and this sends things askew on me. For best results and particularly if you are having issues, sift your flour and/or spoon the flour into your measuring cup to get a more accurate, lighter measure.

- **Warm additional ingredients first.** Cool, dry storage is best for dry ingredients and pantry staples, but if your storage area gets really cold (again, a typical winter issue), or if you store dry goods in the refrigerator or freezer, you might need to let them sit out in your warm kitchen and come up closer to room temperature before you start combining and mixing your bread dough. The flour will be your most likely culprit here because it accounts for the greatest and most influential mass of any given ingredient. With the exception of the water, the temperature and amount of other ingredients aren't usually enough to impact the outcome. If your flour is too cold, it will sap the warmth of your hot liquid and cool down the dough, potentially stunting the yeast and/or inordinately increasing your rise time and possibly causing problems. If this is the case, just think ahead a little, measure out the flour, and let it warm up before you start.

- **Patience.** Rise times given in recipes are for ideal circumstances, and we've talked plenty about the fact that yours might not be. Sometimes a recipe just "acts" differently, so have a little patience and go on about your other business while you wait for your bread to behave. Know that more whole-grain recipes and flours, even some *brands* of flours, just take longer to rise (different natural gluten and sugar contents, etc.). A little wait-and-see can make a big difference and be totally worth the wait.

• **Listen to others**. In the end, we've all had our own bread-baking experiences, our ups and our downs and lots of us have little tips and tricks we've compiled over the years. And yes, that means maybe your mother, grandmother, sister, or brother, too. So, chat it up! Let others know about your bread-baking adventures and see what stories and suggestions they have to share.

• **Try again.** I'm not sure that people really like to hear solutions like this, but the fact is that occasionally, you'll miss something, forget a step, or just have a bad bread-baking day. Before you give up on a recipe, the easiest way to fix it is to try it again and see if something just didn't go right. It might be a pain, but it's a whole lot easier than restocking every ingredient and recreating the proverbial bread wheel!

GOOD FOOD IS WORTH GOOD EFFORT

It's been said before and it's worth saying again: We *all* – every one of us – have failures in baking. Anyone who says they haven't is either just not being honest, or doesn't actually bake. A failed batch or a batch that does less than impress is no reason to give up on great homemade breads, or on baking better breads for you and yours. When your bread fails to rise, chuck it to the chickens (get some chickens if you need to) and give it a new go. *Anyone* can be a home baker. Your next success is just a loaf of delicious bread away!

Many Thanks and Good Baking!

Good food is worth our efforts, both for the flavor and the satisfaction – the satisfaction of knowing that we've allowed ourselves to learn a useful skill and the satisfaction that we've taken the time to improve what we put into our bodies. Finding the time for baking and wholesome cooking and eating may not be as easy as it once was, but every generation has had their load to bear, and when we grow and learn new methods, we truly can find ways to bring back some lost arts and lost ways of living. Eating well and providing better fare on our own are, in fact, lost arts, and so I am glad you have taken the time to explore this cookbook, this baking method, and I hope you enjoy your quick-time bread and dough creations.

Thank you for reading. Here's to you and yours, better eating, and happy baking!

ABOUT THE AUTHOR

Homesteading, house-holding, farming, gardening, being a wife and mother, and yes writing, too, represent the majority of ways Mary Ellen Ward spends her days. Believing in living well and eating well and days that end in a feeling of accomplishment, finding ways to incorporate some of the most valuable old-school ways of life into a busy modern one is what she truly enjoys. She considers herself highly fortunate to be able to do so, and enjoys sharing her knowledge and experiences with others who are similarly inclined. Look for more titles from Mary.

OTHER BOOKS BY MARY ELLEN WARD

Please look for more titles by Mary Ellen Ward on Amazon.com. Visit her author page where you can find a list of all current, new, and upcoming releases by Mary. Be a part of Mary's community of followers and check out pictures she shares, blog posts, important links, her biography, and more.

THE HOMEMADE HOMESTEAD

You can also find Mary Ellen Ward sharing her life, tips, tricks, current projects, and other books and resources at her website, TheHomemadeHomestead.com. To be easily updated with new posts, please subscribe to The Homemade Homestead.
You may also like to email Mary Ward to be added to her contact list. The list will be used *only* to update subscribers of important news, such as new books and interesting happenings. Please rest assured that your contact will be used *only* for updates from this author and her website and will *never* be sold to a third party without your permission!

~ If you have enjoyed this book and/or found any small part of it useful, your honest review will be very much appreciated by both the author and fellow and future readers. Thoughtful reviews help good books to be found! ~
Thank You

DISCLAIMER

Please note that although the author makes suggestions and offers personal experiences and information regarding the shelf life and safety of the recipes as detailed herein, the author can take no responsibility for the safety of the food you prepare and offers this information only as observation and consideration. Please note that ultimately the preparation, safety, and storage of your food depends upon you, and is completely your responsibility. The author of this book is in no way claiming any responsibility for the safety of the food you, your family, or any other person prepares or ingests based upon these instructions or the tips and information included herein. Always remember that good quality products, safe handling, and proper storage are necessary to maintain the integrity and safety of your breads and bread products.

NOTES

NOTES

NOTES

NOTES

Made in the USA
Middletown, DE
22 October 2021